I0153099

"First History of Sacramento City" by Dr. John F. Morse

Commemorative Edition

With a profile of Caroline E. Wenzel
by
Gary Kurutz

An article by Caroline E. Wenzel

And comments by Dr. Bob LaPerriere

Sacramento Book Collectors Club
2018

"First History of Sacramento City" by Dr. John F. Morse
Sacramento Book Collectors Club Commemorative Edition
2018
In partnership with the Sacramento County Historical Society

Copyright © 2018 Sacramento Book Collectors Club

Published in the United States of America

All Rights Reserved. Except as permitted under the U.S. Copyright Act of 1976. No part of this book may be used or reproduced in any manner whatsoever without written permission except in the case of brief quotations embodied in critical articles or reviews.

For additional information contact the editor at:
sacramentobookcollectorsclub@gmail.com.

Library of Congress Control Number: 45009343

ISBN: 978-1-945526-32-9

SBCC Web site: www.sacramentobookcollectors.com

Cover Design and Layout by Lawrence Fox, fox@artfox.us
Edited by Rick Castro
Editors note: Some errors are intentional, to follow the style, punctuation and design of the original.

Photographs from the Collection of the Sacramento Book Collectors Club

CONTENTS

DEDICATION

The members of the Sacramento Book Collectors Club dedicate this book to Dr. Bob LaPerriere. As 2017 President of SBCC, we are grateful to the support that Dr. Bob has given our organization.

Dr. Bob LaPerriere is a retired Kaiser/Permanente Dermatologist. A well respected historian, he serves on many boards and holds many titles. He is Curator of the Sierra Sacramento Valley Museum of Medical History, and on the board of the Sacramento History Alliance and the Sacramento County Historical Society. Dr. Bob was also Founder of the Old City Cemetery Committee, and is the Chair of the Sacramento County Cemetery Advisory Commission. His interest in John F. Morse grew out of research and lectures he's given on Gold Rush medicine.

Lawrence Fox

ACKNOWLEDGEMENT

I am very grateful to the Sacramento Book Collectors Club, with support from the Sacramento County Historical Society, for again reprinting Dr. Morse's History of Sacramento...this time in a very affordable format so his vital and exciting history can be shared with many others. And I am especially grateful to Maryellen Burns for sharing my interest in this publication, and its importance, and pursuing its reprinting.

Dr. Bob LaPerriere

INTRODUCTION

The Sacramento Book Collectors Club was founded by a triumvirate of a schoolteacher, a newspaper man and a second hand dealer. The group met at Hart's Restaurant on 919 K Street at 7pm, Friday, February 10, 1939. Sixteen other book lovers joined them at the meeting. These included a couple of printers, clerks, engineers, an attorney or two, some librarians and housewives. When they decided to organize into a club, an engineer with the State Division of Water Resources, Walter Stoddard was elected president. The teacher, Edward H. Crussell, was elected vice-president, and Edward L. Sterne, city editor of the Sacramento *Union,* was elected secretary. They continued to meet at Hart's Restaurant and at the Hobby Shop on J Street but because of the pressures of World War II, only one was meeting was held between February 1944 and April 1947. The group has met on a regular basis for the last 70 years.

"First History of Sacramento City" by Dr. John F. Morse was first published in 1853 in Colville's *Sacramento City Directory* and reissued by the Sacramento Book Collectors Club in 1945, with an historical note on Dr. Morse's life by Caroline El. Wenzel. It was the third book published by the club, under the direction of George Smisor, the printing instructor at Sacramento Junior College, who used the books as projects for his students during their year's course. His students had not been exposed to printing presses but Smisor accomplished a miracle as he was a great teacher and printer. The first three books were brought out in editions of 180 copies and were attractively bound by Silvius and Schoenbackler, a Sacramento firm of commercial binders.

Since 1945, the club has issued 22 books and more than 700 keepsakes. Most are in the permanent collections of the UC Davis and California State University Sacramento Libraries, the California State Library, UC Davis, and the Sacramento Public Library. SPL features a display case in the Sacramento Room of the Central Library. SBCC has been a member of the Fellowship of American Bibliophilic Societies and was a founding member of the Conference of California Historical Societies and Sacramento County Historical Society.

All this has been accomplished as a labor of love by the SBCC members who have devoted their time, energy and love of books to make the Club's programs a success.

Writing a profile of Caroline E. Wenzel is Gary F. Kurutz. Kurutz has served as Director of the Special Collections Branch of the California State Library in Sacramento. Previously, he held positions as Head Librarian, Sutro Library; Library Director, California Historical Society; and Bibliographer of Western Americana at The Huntington Library.

Kurutz writes California and Western subjects. He is chair of the Collections Committee of the California Historical Society, honorary member of the Society of California Pioneers, and past president of the Book Club of California and SBCC.

"MISS CALIFORNIA"
A PROFILE OF CAROLINE E. WENZEL

By Gary Kurutz

When the *Sacramento Union* for 1945 published a
review of the Sacramento Book Collectors Club new book,

The First History of Sacramento City by Dr. John F. Morse, the anonymous reporter wrote in awe of the meticulous research of Caroline Wenzel who produced the fourteen-page biography of Morse that prefaced his text.[1] The article went on to note that Wenzel had spent close to two years documenting the life of this important Sacramento and California pioneer. The newspaper's high praise is not surprising as Wenzel, over the course of nearly forty years, had developed a reputation as the foremost expert and final authority on California history. She was heralded throughout the Golden State as the doyenne of Californiana and often referred to with the adulatory title of "Miss California."

Caroline Wenzel in '49er dress with two unidentified gentelmen.

Born in San Francisco in 1886, Wenzel moved to Sacramento with her family at the tender age of five. She attended local schools and obtained her college degree from the University of California at Berkeley. As she matured, this budding scholar developed a passion for history and books and decided what better way to express that passion than to become a librarian. She enrolled in the first class of the California State Library School in 1914 when it was under the direction of State Librarian James L. Gillis.[2] At the time, all the students were female and were proudly referred to as "Gillis Girls." Completing her studies, Wenzel landed a job in the State Library, and ten years later, happily joined the library's prestigious California Section. She had the good fortune of working as an assistant to the department's founding librarian, Eudora Garoutte.[3] A native of Woodland, Garoutte was hired by Gillis in 1899 at a pivotal time in the State Library's history. A remarkably farsighted man, Gillis revolutionized California libraries by establishing the county library system, instituting a statewide interlibrary loan program, and opening the vast collections of the State Library to the general public. It was under his powerful direction that the California Section was established. Garoutte organized the unit and put in place many of the policies and procedures that would govern its operation for virtually the entire Twentieth Century. During those years under Garoutte, Wenzel soaked up California history and became the proverbial walking encyclopedia.

In 1933, Garoutte announced her retirement and it was only natural that Wenzel took over as the supervising librarian of the California Section. With the library now located in the stately new Library and Courts Building, Wenzel continued her mentor's legacy. More than anything, she believed in the highest level of public service and gave equal treatment to the tyro researcher or the established scholar. She thoroughly enjoyed the pedagogical role of the librarian. One can only imagine what it was like for a newcomer to walk down that long corridor to the spacious and elegantly decorated California History Room and to be greeted by a smiling and enthusiastic Wenzel, eager to help

California State Library

Over the years, Wenzel expanded her department's collections but, more importantly, greatly enhanced its accessibility. One of the greatest assets added to this gold mine of history was its special index known as the California Information File. Under her direction, Wenzel's staff of one librarian and two clerks added thousands of index cards containing information on people, places, and events in California history. This would include citations from books, periodicals, and newspapers. Arguably, it is the finest data base there is on California history. This, in turn, was supported by the San Francisco Newspaper Index. Both these resources saved library patrons countless hours of tedious searching. In addition, staff typed out obituaries and pertinent articles gleaned from newspapers and periodicals. With her engaging personality, she also convinced researchers to turn over their citations on whatever California subject they were investigating. These she systematically placed into her then famous black binders. With these powerful bibliographic tools, Wenzel answered scores of in-person, telephone, and written requests for California information literally from around the globe.

As brought out in various newspapers, journal articles, and book acknowledgments, Wenzel commanded the respect of everyone studying the state's past. A true scholar, she was a sticker for facts and insisted on accuracy. "Committing an error in history," she remarked, "is like tossing a pebble into the water. Its ripples go on and on." An article in the *Sacramento Bee,* captured a lighter side: "Graced with a pixie like sense of humor, she once said: 'History is a little like a woman — many sides and contradictory. You have to pursue her with a box of chocolates under one arm and a bull whip under the other.'"

With such an agile mind and love of California history, this dynamic librarian naturally became active with various historical and bibliophilic groups foremost of which, of course, was the Sacramento Book Collectors Club. She participated in its meetings and helped with proposed publications. Wenzel, as mentioned above, wrote the detailed biography of pioneer historian Dr. Morse for Publication No. 3, *The First History of Sacramento City* (1945). Five years later in 1950, the Club published its fourth book, a new edition of *Sacramento Illustrated*. To give it context, this handsome quarto came with an "Introductory Note by Caroline Wenzel." In those days, "Introductory Note" was synonymous with exhaustive research consisting of a comprehensive history of the original 1855 Sacramento imprint. Remarkably, she served only as the Club's vice-president in 1953 and never held any other office. Perhaps, her tireless effort in preserving and making accessible California history precluded holding other positions.

Many other organizations called upon her expertise including the California Historical Society, American and California Library associations, American Pioneer Trails Association, Sacramento Historic Landmarks Committee, Sacramento County Historical Society, Sacramento Saturday Club, and the League of Women's Service to name just a few. Because of her esteemed reputation, these groups frequently invited Wenzel to give talks at their meetings and to assist with their publications. On June 16, 1940, for example, she gave a lively presentation to the California Historical Society at the Stanford Mansion in Sacramento entitled "Finding Facts about the Stanfords." The Society published her address in its September 1940 issue of its quarterly.

In the fall of 1952, Wenzel announced her retirement from the State Library following thirty-seven illustrious years of public service and twenty-two years as chief of the California Section.[4] Her announcement, effective December 31, sent tremors through the historical community. Newspapers in Sacramento, San Francisco, Oakland, and Los Angeles published articles celebrating her many contributions. The *Sacramento Union* wrote, "It would be difficult to find an authoritative work on California which does not carry either a preface by her or an acknowledgement of her assistance." Several noteworthy historians of California sent praiseworthy comments. Carl I. Wheat, the distinguished bibliographer and Western map authority said, "You are a maker of authors." History professor Rodman Paul from the California Institute of Technology wrote: "Miss Wenzel's patience is rivaled only by her knowledge of California history," and prolific San Francisco journalist and author, Joseph Henry Jackson likewise applauded her in a three-column article in the January 18, 1953, issue of the *San Francisco Chronicle*. No less an esteemed figure than Governor Earl Warren wrote: "You have reason to take pride in the fact that your efforts have contributed tremendously to the creation of the great fund of knowledge which is now available to all who would know the story of our great state."

B. F. Hastings Building

Now in control of her own time, Wenzel planned to devote herself to writing a history of her beloved city of Sacramento. However, researchers still sought her out and her retirement merely meant a shift from the State Library's reference desk to her home library. Laughingly, she told Harriet Smith of the *Bee*, "I have a collection of books at home which I call my conceit library. I call it that because the authors have mentioned me in their acknowledgements and inscribed the gift books to me." Soon, other related projects distracted her. One of her major contributions was to prove that for thirty-five years Sacramento had designated the wrong building in present day Old Town as the Pony Express headquarters. Through painstaking research she determined that it was the B. F. Hastings Building. Given this level of sleuthing, it is not surprising that the *Sacramento Bee* itself depended on her fact finding and checking for their award-winning *Centennial Album* published in nine parts in its 1957–58 issues.

Regretfully, these challenging tasks and helping others with their research projects absorbed her precious time. In the fall of 1958 a fatal illness struck this grand lady and she passed away on March 24, 1959. Consequently, Wenzel's Sacramento history died with her. As the *Bee* reported "her death shocked her legion of friends and contemporaries in library and historical circles from the Pacific to the Atlantic." The extraordinary outpouring of grief served as powerful and eloquent testimony of the vital importance of this librarian-historian. Journals and newspapers spread the sad news lamenting the loss of perhaps the greatest human resource ever on the state's history. One admirer wrote, "To authors and to historians, she is – and always will be – 'Miss California.'"

Fortunately, others perpetuated her memory. Less than a month after her death, the California Historical Society announced the establishment of the Caroline Wenzel Scholarship to support research in Western history and librarianship. The *Sacramento Bee* initiated the fund with a generous donation of $1,000. Federal Judge Sherrill Halbert, one of her close friends, served as the fund's chair and reported that a "steady flow of contributions" had been received. An even more moving and lasting tribute emerged. Under construction in today's Greenhaven-Pocket neighborhood of Sacramento was a new elementary school. Led by the *Sacramento Bee* and a legion of researchers, a successful campaign was undertaken to have the school named in her honor. On May 27, 1970, at 4:00

PM, the Sacramento Unified School District dedicated the Caroline Wenzel Elementary School. Appropriately, Judge Halbert gave the dedicatory address. Caroline's sister, Florine Wenzel, presented the school with a Sacramento City flag in her memory. Wenzel's life and career, as expressed by this new educational facility, would inspire in young people a love and interest in the history of their own city and state. What a rare tribute to have a school named for a librarian!

It is only fitting, then, that the Sacramento Book Collectors Club continue Wenzel's legacy by publishing this new and elegant edition of Sacramento's first history complete with her brilliantly researched biography of Dr. John F. Morse.

Endnotes

1.

The *Sacramento Union* article appeared in its October 14, 1945 issue. Material for this short profile has been gathered from the Caroline Wenzel Biographical File, a scrapbook of articles and clippings about her life, and the Caroline Wenzel Collection consisting of twenty-six boxes of her correspondence, clippings, speeches, and research notes. All are in the California History Section, California State Library.

2.

For a history of the California State Library School see Robert D. Harlan, "California State Library Library School: 1914-1921." *California State Library Foundation Bulletin*, 9:12–13. The school closed when the University of California at Berkeley established its library school.

3.

For a short biography of Eudora Garroute see Gary F. Kurutz, "Eudora Garoutte, Doyenne of California History Librarian," *California State Library Foundation Bulletin*, 115, 2015, pp. 28-31.

4.

Fortunately for the historical community and the State Library, Alan R. Ottley succeeded Wenzel as the California Section's supervising librarian. Ottley was an active member of the Sacramento Book Collectors Club.

FINDING FACTS ABOUT THE STANFORDS IN THE CALIFORNIA STATE LIBRARY

By CAROLINE WENZEL Supervising Librarian,
California Section, California State Library

An Address before the California Historical Society Delivered at the Stanford Mansion in Sacramento on June 16, 1940. (This address by Caroline Wenzel opens with a detailed explanation of the workings of the California section of the State Library, then discusses the history of the Leland Stanford mansion in Sacramento.)

It is indeed a pleasure to have the privilege of speaking in such an historic setting to the members of the California Historical Society and their guests.

In my childhood days I frequently passed the Stanford home on my way to school and I often wished that I might enter the house and see with my own eyes the home in which Governor and Mrs. Stanford once entertained so lavishly, and especially did I want to see the room where young Leland was born. The house was not open to visitors then and, for some reason or other, I never had the courage to go up to the door and ask the good sister to let me enter. Once the kindly gardener made me happy by giving me some of the lovely violets that grew in such profusion in the yard. The place still interests me, and now, from the windows of the California Room of the Library I can point with pride to the historic house and tell visitors that they are welcome to visit the home during certain hours of the day, thanks to the hospitality of Sister Lucile and her staff.

I know that you are all interested in hearing something about the history of the house and the changes that have been made in it, but before speaking of this I want to tell something about the California Section of the State Library. After all, that is the only reason for my appearing before you, because you all know that I am better as a literary detective in the field of Californiana than as a public speaker.

The State Library was established in 1850, and the acquisition of California material actually began at that time. The California Section, however, was not organized as such until 1903. The Library, which was then housed in the State Capitol, had throughout its collection, books, magazines, and newspapers which were either printed in California or pertained to the State. The California Section was created by bringing together this scattered material as one collection. Since that time the resources of the department have been steadily increased and its usefulness extended until today it is known to collectors, research workers, and writers throughout the country.

In the California Room are located the rare and most important reference books and the various catalogues and indices maintained as special units of our work.

The staff of the California Section consists of two professional librarians, a newspaper indexer and two library aids. The work is highly specialized and entails much hard work both in and out of library hours, but if one is interested in it there is a glamour and thrill about it that is difficult to describe. We are a vital part of the community. Our public is interested chiefly in the early history and literature of our State, but there is also a wide interest in the history of its art, music, religion, politics, economics, agriculture and allied subjects, so we must have information easily available about material pertaining to these subjects and especially must we be alert to references to current California events and books.

The aim of the State Library is to provide supplementary material to the libraries of the State and to lend to individuals through their local libraries. We try to adhere to this policy, but in the case of writers and research workers, when we know that the material is not in book form and not available elsewhere, we sometimes send the information direct to the individual. This applies particularly to people outside of the State.

Original material, newspapers, certain periodicals, reference books, and books that would be difficult or impossible to replace do not leave the library. If an applicant is unable to come to Sacramento to obtain information from a newspaper or book that does not circulate, we make photostats to a limited extent at a nominal cost for designated items.

We do a limited amount of searching in newspapers for such items as births, marriages, deaths and biographical sketches, when we do not find references in the information file, and these articles, if not too lengthy, are typed free of charge. We are quite willing to extend this search to books and other sources when the question is a difficult and important one which the local librarian is not able to answer because of limited reference tools.

Requests sometimes come to us concerning subjects

which would require more specialized research than we have the time to do. In such cases we suggest that the student himself come to the State Library, if possible, and do his research work here. This individual service is a very important part of our work, and we are always glad to make all material available and give every possible assistance.

The book collection includes books on the history and description, resources and industries of the State, as well as the works of California authors in all departments of literature. The work of our fine printers is also represented.

A unique feature of the California collection and one that we believe is as complete as any of its kind in existence is that of California fiction. Books with a California setting or by a California author are included in this group. Many of them are autographed and are the gift of the author. Since it has been found that no other class of literature disappears as rapidly as popular fiction, these books are kept as a representative collection of this type of literature through the various periods of the State's history.

The collection of county histories includes nearly all which have been published. These volumes, especially the early ones, contain much valuable biographical I and historical material and, supplemented by early directories and great registers of voters, they serve as useful reference tools, especially since the biographical sketches in county histories have been indexed in card form. The directories and great registers of voters are also valuable in helping to establish proof of citizenship and in verifying age and residence in this State, particularly for those needing proof for old age pension claims.

An interesting and valuable collection of California periodicals includes complete files of the Pioneer, the first magazine of importance published in the State, the Hesperian, the first magazine illustrated in color, and also complete files of the Overland, Hutchings, Californian and the Argonaut.

The manuscript collection consists of early mission documents, business papers, diaries, letters and reminiscences of pioneers, as well as biographical cards of California authors, artists, musicians, state officials, pioneers and early settlers. As no other material gives a better idea of the true character and spirit of the men and women who came to California, we have listed the letters both by the names of the person and by date, thus assuring the greatest possible use.

Several thousand pictures have been collected, portraying persons, places and events in California history.

A theatrical collection consisting of actors' photographs, playbills, programs, biographical information, manuscripts and printed copies of the work of California players is one of the special features of the department.

Aside from the very definite types of material already listed, there is much in the miscellaneous collection, including old account books, scrapbooks, early ballots and political dodgers, bookplates, sheet music, concert programs and the like.

Perhaps the California Section is better known for its unsurpassed collection of newspapers of the State than for anything else. The file begins with the first paper, the Californian, which started in Monterey on August 15, 1846, and includes nearly every representative paper from that time until the present. Nearly all the early San Francisco papers, such as the California Star, the Alta California, the Herald and the Bulletin, as well as many northern papers, including the Placer Times, the Sacramento Union and the Sacramento Bee, are in the collection. These newspapers, now numbering over sixteen thousand volumes, are bound and shelved by counties in the specially constructed newspaper stacks and are listed in a card catalogue by title and locality. At the present time over two hundred California papers are received regularly and about ten from outside the State. Needless to say, these papers do not circulate.

One of the most useful tools in the department is a card index to California material found in California newspapers. The index covers the period from 1846 to date, and the entries, estimated at over five million, are chiefly from San Francisco papers with the exception of about thirty-five thousand cards which were indexed by Winfield Davis from the Sacramento Union. This index is of great assistance in locating sketches of California people and places and items of local historical interest. Frequently people come into the Library and tell us they understand that we have a subject index to all the newspapers published in California, but such is not the case. At the present time the San Francisco Chronicle is the only newspaper being indexed, and it takes the full time of the newspaper indexer to keep it up to date. Only California items are indexed, and legal notices and advertisements are not included.

In addition to the newspaper index and the general dictionary catalogue of California books, several other card catalogues are maintained in the California Room. The information catalogue consists of miscellaneous references to material that has been found in county histories, periodicals, directories, general books, etc. Entries to this index are being constantly added, thus widening its scope and increasing its value.

Perhaps I can best give you an idea of how this material is used by telling you of the assistance we were able to give to the citizens of Sacramento last year when the Centennial was celebrated. Much interest was aroused in the community. Stories of the pioneer days were recalled and old songs and dramas revived. A local newspaper, the Sacramento Bee, published a guidebook, and a group of merchants sponsored a series of broadcasts featuring stories of local interest. Guests invited to many of the large balls and parties that were given were requested to wear costumes of the 1839 period, and we were kept busy advising them regarding the styles and furnishing photostatic copies of costumes to the dressmakers.

Some of the local citizens decided that it would be a good idea to assist in the work of renovating the old Stanford mansion and have it open for inspection during the Centennial celebration. This naturally aroused curiosity regarding the house and its early occupants. The public turned to the State Library for information.

Although the Stanfords were married in 1850, and Mr. Stanford came to California in 1857, it was not until 1855 that Mrs. Stanford came to make her home in Sacramento. At that time there was no suitable dwelling for rent, so they lived in a hotel until a small house on Second Street between O and P Streets became vacant. They furnished this house in a very frugal manner, and Mrs. Stanford did her own housekeeping.

Wealth and distinction came to the Stanfords during their stay in Sacramento. It was here, at 54 K Street, that the Big Four—Stanford, Crocker, Huntington and Hopkins—conceived and carried into successful execution the daring scheme of building a transcontinental railroad. Also very important to us is the fact that these same men were all charter life members of the Sacramento Library Association, which later became the Sacramento Public Library.

The Stanfords entertained frequently in the days of their growing wealth and growing popularity. Yet for all their prominence, only brief mention is to be found in books of the home life of the Stanfords during their residence in Sacramento. Considering the vast amount of material that has been published about them this is rather surprising. After exhausting the references in our indexes we found it necessary to make a diligent search of newspapers, directories, county records, etc., for information.

The first item we located read as follows:

GUBERNATORIAL MANSION.-Leland Stanford purchased yesterday of S. C. Fogus the house and lot on the southeast corner of Eighth and N streets, for the sum of $8,000. The property consists of two full lots— a quarter of a block—with a two-story brick dwelling house, finished in a costly manner inside and out, with addition of frame building, brick stable, fruit trees, shrubbery, etc., surrounding it.

The article appeared in the Sacramento Union of July 12, 1861, and the caption:

"GUBERNATORIAL MANSION" is optimistic, to say the least, because Stanford, though nominated for governor on June 19th of that year, was not elected until September 4.

From the records in the assessor's office it was found that the house was originally built between the years 1857 and 1858 by Shelton C. Fogus, a wholesale merchant and one time city councilman of Sacramento. It was sold to Stanford for less than the 1858 assessed valuation.

In 1872, just after the mansion had been renovated, the assessment against Stanford included $45,000 for improvements and $1,000 for a library. In addition to his other assessments there was listed against him the following personal property: 11 vehicles, $3,000; 12 mares, $3,500; 4 horses, $1,500; 1 horse [probably "Occident"], $20,000; 2 colts, $150, and 2 cows, $100

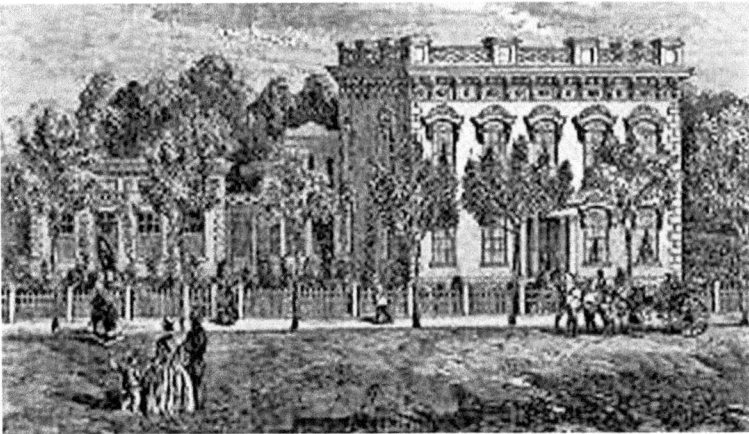

The following description of the mansion by Colonel James Lloyd La Fayette Warren, who restored the grounds after the flood, appeared in the California Farmer of July 4, 1862:

"...The mansion itself can be said to be the most perfect specimen of a residence in this State, the main building is 46 by 40, with a wing in the rear of 20 feet by 31. another wing to which is attached the Governor's office, is 32 feet by 18. The office of the Governor is furnished with reference to convenience of business, yet with taste and neatness. it contains the department for clerks and his private office, the whole complete in itself, easily communicating with his dwelling. The whole design forms a unique and faultless structure.

The saloons on each side of the hall occupy the whole size of the building, and are lofty and elegant, being 16 feet high. The side centers are ornamented with chaste Corinthian columns and caps, with architraves over the doors, these, with rich central ornaments of pure white for the chandeliers, make a fine contrast to the oak-grained wood-work, and give to the whole an elegant appearance. The chambers, also, are the entire size of the building, but making four in number, are 14 feet high, furnished perfectly, with blinds and shades so as to control both heat and light.

The mansion, to the view, is lofty, having a heavy rich cornice and coping for each window and ornaments under the cornice. [Parenthetically let me say that on each of the ornamented windows the head of a man is carved, and up to the present time we have not been able to determine who is represented. I throw this out as a challenge to the historians gathered here.] The front entrance is furnished with Corinthian columns and caps. The outside of the building (being of brick, with extra solid foundations) is finished in blocks and painted a delicate stone color; cornices and copings a lead color, which present a soft yet delicate tint. Yet the whole is much more beautiful in its natural view, than any illustrations can make it...."

In front of the mansion a noble liberty pole, 116 feet high, was raised, and from its point waved the Stars and Stripes—a banner 30 feet long.

Beautiful gardens surrounded the building, but they were destroyed by the flood of 1861-62.

It was owing to this flood that the inauguration ceremonies incidental to Stanford's assuming the office of governor were made as brief as possible.

On January 10, 1862, the day of the inauguration, flood waters swept Sacramento. The Governor-elect went to the capitol, at that time on I Street at Seventh, in a row boat, and when he returned home a few hours later, the water was so deep, he had to enter the house through a second story window. In those days the house that now stands three stories high was but two. It was not until ten years later that the building was raised and what is now the ground floor placed beneath.

Ella Sterling Mighels, who knew the Governor as a tiny child, once wrote that her father said that the waters rose and surrounded the house, and everyone left the city who could. Governor Stanford's mansion was abandoned. But in the midst of the worries of everybody, there was seen a poor cow in the drawing room of the mansion, with her head sticking out of the window and mooing incessantly for help. finally a boat went up alongside and pitched in some hay for her and she settled down peacefully in her headquarters.

The story has been told that the piano was floating about in the reception room on the lower floor. Being a bit skeptical about this story, we tried to verify it in contemporary papers, but were not able to do so. However, we did find one article that stated that the piano in the parlor of the Chief Justice of the Supreme Court, though perched on chairs, was soaked and probably rendered worthless, and that the pictures in the parlor of the new Governor were spoiled.

Mrs. Stanford actively participated in the social affairs of Sacramento, and in an article in the San Francisco Alta California, of February 23, 1863, we find a notice which states that ladies will be interested to understand a new rule of etiquette lately decreed by Mrs. Governor Stanford, with the concurrence of the wives of various officials of the city. This rule was that Mrs. Stanford would expect the first call from ladies visiting Sacramento. This rule had become a matter of necessity because so many wives of members of the legislature came to the capital to spend a few days, and the Governor's wife would like to call upon them, but she did not know when they were in the city or where they stopped. Evidently there was objection to this new procedure, because the article explained in great length that it was based on a rule well established in Washington and other places.

We found that many notables were entertained in this house during the time the Stanfords lived here.

The most brilliant affair that occurred was the magnificent ball given in February 1872, in honor of Governor Newton Booth and the members of the legislature. A San Francisco newspaper sent a special reporter to the party, and a three-column description was telegraphed to the paper. The headlines would have captured the fancy of a Hollywood producer of today.

The party was given just after the mansion had been thoroughly renovated, the house had been raised, a lower floor and mansard roof constructed, additional wings built, and altogether its appearance radically changed.

In order that you may visualize the home as it was at that time, I will read, with your permission, excerpts from the description that appeared in the Chronicle of February 7, 1872:

"...It [the mansion] contains forty-four rooms, all most elaborately and luxuriously furnished and fitted up. Good taste and cultured imaginations have been exhausted in furnishing the establishment. Magnificent and costly furniture in every room; lace curtains of the finest fabric; carpets that receive with noiseless tread the footfall; frescoes beautiful in design and exquisite in artistic perfection, adorn the wars and ceiling. Large bouquets of natural flowers are placed in every room, and their fragrance perfumes the air. Added to these are numerous baskets of artificial flowers, pendent from which artificial birds warble forth the rarest music, imitating canaries and other sweet singers. These artificial birds are an ingenious piece of mechanism, winding up like a clock. It requires an expert to say that they are not live birds. The bedroom and adjacent apartment in which the supper is served present a most inviting appearance. For each guest there are six different wine glasses. The entire service, from napkin-rings to centerpieces, is of solid silver, all being entirely new. There is room for 200 guests at a sitting. [From] the sidewalk to the grand entrance of the mansion is a waterproof canopy. Ladies descending from carriages are thus protected from rain, and an elegant carpet adds to the comfort. Everything is on a scale of unsurpassed magnificence.

Seven hundred invitations were issued by the hospitable Stanfords, principally to their friends and acquaintances, who were asked to come and make themselves it home. Of these five hundred were issued to friends in Sacramento; the others to those in San Francisco....

On entering the mansion of the Stanfords the guests were escorted upstairs, where appropriate dressing rooms had being prepared wherein the ladies could prepare themselves for the general muster and the gentlemen give their claw-hammers the last graceful touch. Being so prepared, and everything in apple-pie order, the guests descend. In the parlors to the right as you enter Mr. and Mrs. Leland Stanford receive their guests. The Governor looks pleasant, and has a hearty greeting for all his friends. Mrs. Stanford looks radiant, and feels happy at the idea that this, her grand reception, is a grand success in every sense of the word. She has pleasant words for the ladies and vies with the Governor in exchanging compliments. The guests then pass on to the other apartments.

The disciples of Terpsichore soon find where they can worship at their favored shrine. Church & Clark of Sacramento furnish the music. Seven pieces are stationed in the parlors to the left which connect with a large hall 30 by 86. The parlors are 20 by 50. The second band is stationed on the lower floor in the hall beneath the main upper hall. This lower hall is also 30 by 86. This gives, according to our hurried mathematics, 6,000 square feet of space covered with the tireless dancers...."

For those of you who might be interested in knowing about the order of dances, the menu, the names of those present, and a description of the gowns worn by the ladies, a photostatic copy of the Chronicle article is on display in an exhibition case in the State Library. Mayhap one of you will find the name of a member of your family among the list of guests.

It was in this house that Leland Stanford, Jr., was born on a sunny day in May 1868. This to both Mr. and Mrs. Stanford was the crowning event of their lives. They had been married eighteen years and had not before been blessed with a child.

You are all familiar with the story told by Bertha Berner in her biography of Mrs. Leland Stanford, that shortly before the birth of young Leland Mr. and Mrs. Stanford and a group of friends were enjoying a tea party out of doors on the front veranda. Mrs. Stanford, sitting in a rocking chair, overbalanced and tipped off the porch into a flowering bush. Her husband was stunned, but Mrs. Stanford was rescued without mishap and laughingly assured them that she was not hurt in the least."

Miss Berner also tells this story:

When the baby was only a few weeks old, Mr. Stanford asked Mrs. Stanford to arrange a dinner party for a group of their particular friends. It was a large party, and when they were seated the waiter brought in a large silver platter with a cover and placed it in the center of the table. Mrs. Stanford was very much surprised, for she had planned nothing of the sort and also had not seen the platter before. Then Mr. Stanford arose and said, "My friends, I wish now to introduce my son to you!" When the cover of the silver dish was lifted, the baby was discovered lying in it on blossoms. He was carried around the table and shown to each guest. He was smiling, and went through introduction very nicely.

The platter, beautifully engraved, now reposes on the sideboard with other pieces of an elaborate silver service.

Mrs. Mighels recalled memories of Mrs. Stanford driving with her mother and sister, Miss Lathrop, and said that when the little boy was taken along, he looked like a baby prince, he was so bedecked and so cherished, as if he were more than an ordinary child. He had dark eyes and resembled his mother and his aunt more than his father. As he grew, he was very fond of playing at railroading, so a track was built for him and he was given a little car to run on it.

The son was six years of age when the family moved to San Francisco. His death in Florence, Italy, at the age of sixteen, was the cause of great grief to his parents

Leland Stanford Jr. in 1872

Mr. Stanford's beloved mother lived with them for a time and died here in February 1873.

When the Stanfords moved to San Francisco in 1874 they left the home in Sacramento completely furnished. Mrs. Stanford always kept a very warm spot in her heart for Sacramento and frequently remembered the city with generous gifts in later years. On February 7, 1888, she sent a check from Washington, D.C. for the Protestant Orphan Asylum. On April 25, 1890, in keeping with her creedless religious ideals, she sent $1,000 to the mayor with the request that the sum be distributed among the more worthy charities of the city. That same year she had placed in St. Paul's Episcopal Church a magnificent memorial window of stained glass, said to be at that time the most costly in this country or Europe. A few years later she presented to the Cathedral of the Blessed Sacrament a magnificent painting of Raphael's Sistine Madonna, copied by permission from the Royal Gallery in Dresden. She also contributed a sum of money to assist in the purchase of Sutter's Fort.

On April 18, 1900, she came to Sacramento to make a final disposal of the mansion where her happiest days had been spent and her loved son born. For twenty years this home had been unoccupied, save for a solitary caretaker who had served in that capacity since Senator and Mrs. Stanford had removed to San Francisco. Before leaving for a prolonged stay in Europe, Mrs. Stanford wished to safeguard for all time the cherished place and its sacred memories. Money could not buy the "old home," and love forbade that it should ever be given over to profane use. Therefore, she offered to the Most Reverend Thomas Grace, Bishop of Sacramento, and his successors in the bishopric, forever, the home, together with an endowment of $75,000. The Bishop, honoring the charity and lovable intentions of Mrs. Stanford, accepted the gift, and promised that the hallowed spot should be preserved according to her wishes.

When going through the building you will notice evidence of the railroad builders interest. Two crystal light shades on a chandelier in the banquet room remain of all those that bore etched designs of an engine resembling the famed "C. P. Huntington." Again, the railroad design appears in Stanford's own glass enclosed bookcase. At the top, the engine and one car are carved, and the initial "S" appear on both frosted glass doors of the case.

In conclusion, may I say that we are still seeking information about the Stanfords. No doubt, there are invitations, photographs, original letters, etc., concerning them in the possession of individuals. It is our earnest hope that this material will be brought to the attention of the Library or the Historical Society in order that the information may be made available to future historians.

California Historical Society Quarterly
September 1940

A PERSPECTIVE OF MEDICINE IN THE 1800'S
AND DR. JOHN F. MORSE
By Dr. Bob LaPerriere

There is little relation between medicine as practiced today and two centuries ago. The main evolution was from treating the patient to treating the disease. Physical diagnosis is the only common thread...and a thread that is unraveling due to today's dependence on technology.

To get a real perspective of medicine in the 1800's I will share a portion of a letter written in 1825, given to me by one of my patients.

> On the sixth of Sept. I was seriously attacked with a billious fever, also threatened with a dropsy.
>
> My Physician thought it impossible for me to bear a run of the fever, he commenced breaking it on Sunday by bleeding and puking, which was continued on Monday.
>
> I was partially deranged on Sunday which was followed by a state of mental madness caused by excruciating pain about the crown of my head, of the most agonizing torture that experience could conceive or tongue describe. I had my head shaved and blistered one also upon my neck, upon my back, upon my bowels one upon each arm, one upon each leg, eight in number all sore at a time, very large and inflamed, yet the chief evidence I have of the existence is the scars upon my body, a partial derangement succeeded madness.
>
> Three months are lost to me. Time appears like an almost forgotten dream. I must turn from this subject, the recollection of it chills my blood. I view this affliction as a punishment for an abuse of reason. My nerves are still irritable. My health is tolerably good.

This was a time when medical treatments consisted of physical modalities such as cupping, bleeding, puking and purging, and pharmaceuticals featured arsenic, mercury, strychnine and narcotics. Surgery, largely amputation, was done without anesthesia until the late 1850's...and opening the abdomen was not done until the late 1800's, and it was also not until the 1880's that aseptic surgery was introduced, minimizing life threatening infections.

These shortcomings in early medical care are reflected in the following excerpt from a document written in 1922, by an Auburn physician, reflecting on his prior 50 years in medicine:

The patient was a young Scotchman who had just arrived at the local hotel with his wife whom he had married before leaving the old country, and who knew no word excepting Gaelic. He came with a few pounds in cash, intending to buy a farm and become a settler.

He was almost at once stricken with what was, no doubt, an attack of appendicitis, in the face of which the profession then stood helpless, calling it "peritonitis" and keeping the unfortunate under the influence of opium until death closed the tragedy.

The scene at the bedside has haunted me throughout the years. The man lay gasping out the last of his life, and his young wife knelt by the bedside with her arms outflung across his body, and her face buried therein, crying out in rhythmical cadence Gaelic words...the despairing cry of a broken heart in a new world, without friends, and even without knowledge of the language spoken around her.

Without knowledge of the cause of most diseases, and no recognition of the existence of microbes, physicians had to be content with treating the patient rather than treating the disease. The doctor had virtually none of the tools that are necessary today to make a proper diagnosis...and even if he did, specific medications for various diseases and antibiotics were at least a half-century away. It was rather amazing how a physician in the 1800's could function...making house calls by horse and buggy in addition to managing office hours, sometimes even in the evening, and in the case of Dr. Morse, carefully describing the evolution of this river city over several years

It was not unusual for a patient's inability to pay his doctor, especially during the gold rush; so many physicians need other sources of income, as was the case with Dr. Morse. He entered into banking and real estate. He was the first editor of the Sacramento Daily Union, a member of the Board of Directors of Central Pacific Railroad, and an original staff member of Toland Medical College in San Francisco. He additionally co-founded the first agricultural paper on the Pacific Coast, was a volunteer fireman, served as temporary chairman of the group, which formed the California Medical Association, edited the California State Medical Journal and was vice president of the California Prison Commission. And he was one of the originators of the Sacramento County Medical Society.

Dr. Morse graphically described mid 19th Century Sacramento, whether it was a sad and depressing event or a joyous and uplifting one. Here are excerpts illustrating both these endeavors. Dr. Morse's description of a Pioneer, enveloped in a blanket, rescued from the first floor of a building used as a hospital, during a flood and who was close to death:

The blanket was, with difficulty, detached, and when drawn off presented a shirtless body partially devoured by an immense bed of maggots occupying nearly as much space as the emaciated carcass itself. And when one adds to this loathsome mass, these crawling elements of disgust, the accumulated excretions which were alike confined by the agglutinated folds of the blanket, a head of hair almost clogged up with vermin, then can a just conception be formed of what was suffered during the sickness of the fall and winter of 1849.

And to be more upbeat and optimistic, I hope you enjoy this description of the 4th of July grand ball at the City Hotel:

> It was essentially important that every Caucasian descendant of Eve in this section of the state should be present. Accordingly a respectable number of gallant young gentlemen were commissioned to explore the country, with specific instructions to visit every ranch, tent, or wagon bed where there was any indication of feminine divinity, and irrespective of age, cultivation, or grace, to bring one and all to this aristocratic festivity at the opening of the dance the hungry, rather voracious optics of about two hundred plain looking gentlemen were greeted with the absolute presence of some eighteen ladies, not amazons all, but replete with all the adornments that belong to bold and enterprising pioneers of a new country.
> Such a sight in California at that time was almost a miraculous exhibition and filled men with such an ebullition of sentiment as to make it impossible to breathe without inhaling the dying cadences of the most devoted and tenderly expressed politeness. Tickets of admission to this ball were $32. The supper was most sumptuously prepared, and champagne circulated so freely that identity became jeopardized and the very illumination of the room converted into a grand magnifying medium for the revels of fancy and delights of illusion. (p. 38-39)

As you can see, Dr. Morse was an accomplished and graphic author. He was also active in the Oddfellows and with the Masons fitted up a hospital in Sutter's Fort in 1849. He strongly advocated the adoption of stringent measures to correct the filthy conditions of the streets and was the first to inaugurate a system of health insurance in California.... for $100 the subscriber was entitled to be attended free at the Oddfellows and Masons Hospital for one year. Dr. Morse then entered into banking and real estate, was the first editor of the Sacramento Daily Union, a member of the Board of Directors of Central Pacific Railroad, and also an original staff member of Toland Medical College in San Francisco. He additionally co-founded the first agricultural paper on the Pacific Coast, was a volunteer fireman, served as temporary chairman of the group that formed the California Medical Association, edited the California State Medical Journal and was vice president of the California Prison Commission. He was one of the originators of the Sacramento County Medical Society. The fact he was well liked and respected was evidenced by the fact that 10,000 people attended his funeral. The involvement by Dr. Morse is representative of the community involvement of many of our early Physicians.

OBITUARY OF DR. JOHN F. MORSE.

Birth 27 December1815
Death 30 December 1874

No man has ever died in California leaving a larger circle of warmly-attached personal friends than Dr. John F. Morse, whose death occurred in San Francisco on the 30th of December.

. Dr. Morse was born in Vermont in 1816. He was educated as a physician, and pursued his medical studies with that ardor and enthusiasm which characterized him in all his undertakings. His profession was ever his pride and his delight. He loved it for the "opportunities for good" which it afforded, and which he never neglected to improve and for the knowledge it conferred on the most interesting and mysterious questions of natural science.

Few men have had a larger or more laborious practice, but he continued as a student to the time of his death, and he leaves no one in the State more thoroughly and familiarly acquainted with medical literature and science, their history, researches and latest results. Latterly, he was especially interested in all investigations into the subtle relations between material and mental phanomena.

He came to California from Brooklyn (where he was a charter member of Plymouth Church) in 1849, arriving on the ship Humboldt, on which he acted as surgeon from Acapulco to San Francisco, and immediately settled in Sacramento.

In the fall of that year, in connection with Dr. Stillman, he opened a hospital at the corner of X and Third streets, on the lot now occupied by Nathan clothing store.

It is impossible for those who were not here to realize, or even for those who were to recall, the professional labors performed and gratuitous services rendered by Dr. Morse in the

Spring of 1850, when the city was inundated ; in the Summer, when it was filled with immigrants, often sick and destitute, and in the Fall, when it was scourged by the cholera. His constitution, not naturally robust, was impaired by constant labor and frequent exposure, and when the Sacramento Union was projected, in March, 1851, be was offered the position of editor, which he accepted, and held for about a year.

Resuming his profession he continued in active practice in this city until 1863, when he removed to San Francisco. His practice was at all times large, generally limited only by his own strength. In the sick room he was one of the kindest and most sympathetic of men, and each of his patients seemed to be the object of a much care and solicitude as though he had but one.

He was also a man of great public spirit, taking a lively interest in every question which affected the community, the State, and the nation. With unusual fluency of speech, and a rapid, impetuous delivery, he was very often called upon for addresses on public occasions, and he became widely known through the State. He was one of the leading Odd Fellows on the Pacific coast, and during a visit to Germany in 1870 he introduced the order into that "empire".

He spent a great portion of the last five years of his life in traveling on account of failing health. He had uniformly found a voyage beneficial, and about two months ago took passage for Australia.

His friends were apprehensive his strength was not sufficient for the journey, and they were right. He went no further than the Hawaiian Islands, and returning reached home a few days before his death. The peculiar and most marked characteristics of his mind and disposition were an ardor that was impulsive, and a devotion that was heroic The friends that he loved "he grappled with books of steel," and he followed his convictions wherever they led. If tender regrets, kind memories, and grateful recollections could build his monument, no man's would rise higher.

Sacramento Daily Union, January 1, 1875

1

RESOLUTIONS IN RESPECT TO THE MEMORY OF
DOCTOR JOHN F. MORSE

Sacramento Pioneer Association President from 1857 to 1859

When a good man dies the world has cause to mourn. His loss appeals to the hearts of all as a common bereavement. A life of zealous devotion to the welfare of mankind. Of earnest and unceasing toil for the accomplishment of good wherever good may be done, of generous and unselfish sympathy with those who suffer from misfortune or wrong everywhere, with a courage and strength to battle against the evils which afflict society and the body politic, and to strike boldly in the interests of our common humanity against every species of outrage and wrong; a life like this when stricken from the roll of being leaves a marked void in the ranks of human benefactors, and in the hearts of those who loved and honored him for his noble worth. The benefactors of mankind are every man's kindred, and men love to dwell upon their memories. The world needs such spirits to keep the embers of philanthropy aglow, to infuse warmth and generous sentiment into the social elements and to dispell the inertia too often consequent upon the absorption of the public mind in the business affairs of life. Such men are Gods stewards everywhere and man most faithful ministers.

Of such was our lamented Brother Doctor John F. Morse. Gifted with talents of a high order, with a noble integrity of character, unflinching courage in the discharge of every duty, ever restless in pursuit of new fields of usefulness; charitable in his professional services to the poor; enthusiastic in the pursuit of knowledge in his profession, with high standing in the councils of the faculty; honored with rank and distinction the several charitable organizations of which he was a member;

intrusted with an important mission to a foreign state for the interest of a great social and beneficial society in which he achieved signal distinction; remembered by the Pioneers as "the good Samaritan" who during the terrible epidemic of 1850, visited from tent to tent regardless of danger, voluntarily administering relief to the suffering who were strangers in a strange land, without friends or kindred, remembered by all as a loss to literature, science, Society, and the social relations which endeared him to life. Therefore

Resolved. That in the decease of our former President and distinguished fellow citizen John F. Morse M.D. our Society has suffered an irreparable loss, and Society at large one of its most noble and brilliant ornaments.

Resolved. That we deeply sympathize with the bereaved family of our deceased brother in their affliction, and tender them our earnest and heartfelt sympathies.

Resolved. That in furtherer token of respect for his memory, these resolutions be entered in full upon the records of this Society and that a copy be sent to the widow and family of the deceased Brother under signature of the President, attested by the Seal and signature of the Secretary of the Society.

W. C. Fitch

Ira E. Oatman

A. B. Nixon

(Resolution after 1874)

THE FIRST
HISTORY OF
SACRAMENTO CITY

Written in 1853 by
JOHN FREDERICK MORSE, M.D.

With a Historical Note on the Life of Dr. Morse,
by CAROLINE WENZEL

Sacramento Book Collectors Club
Sacramento, California
Mcmxlv

Copyright, 1945, by
The Sacramento Book Collectors Club

Printed in the United States of America

Publication No. 3
The Sacramento Book Collectors Club

PREFACE

The *First History of Sacramento* was written by Dr. John F.
Morse and was published in Colville's *Sacramento City Directory* of
October 1853. The town, eldest child of the gold rush, was not yet five
years old, but it was aged beyond its years, and established citizens
already spoke of '49 as of the long ago. To thousands of fortune
hunters, long separated from old haunts and old friends, Sacramento
was the final jumping-off place for the mines and was the convenient
resort for trade, amusement, and dissipation. Speculators in goods,
services, and real estate found the city itself a mine of gold, paying its
dividends, much as did the river placers, according to the dictates of
luck and nature and the stamina and skill of the individual. A booming
frontier town, Sacramento oscillated between inflation and panic, fire
and flood, salubrity and plague. Its early history expresses a world of
diverse interests and transcends that of a single place.

Dr. Morse was one of the city's pioneer settlers and first
citizens. Though a medical man by profession, there were few
movements of the day which did not claim his attention and add to his
reputation. Urged on by a driving energy and enthusiasm, he first tried
the mines, then became editor and publisher, politician and public
servant, lecturer and professor; he was banker, auctioneer, real estate
agent, and promoter. Qualified both as eye-witness and performer, he
could write with authority, and his *History* has long been an
acknowledged source book on the era of the gold rush.

Morse's *History of Sacramento* illustrates many of the personal
characteristics of the man. It shows him a keen and intelligent
observer, a vigorous and sociable personality, marked by sentimentality
and a New England conservatism. Unsympathetic to views and mores
not his own, he was unfalteringly generous wherever there was human

need. A recognized leader in the medical profession, his medical philosophy was progressive for his time. Morse exposed a characteristic aspect of his personality when he announced that his *History* was a preliminary sketch to precede a more complete work on the Sacramento Valley; often his initial enthusiasm did not suffice to carry to completion projects suggested by his lively imagination.* Initiative, energy, and courage were his leading traits. His style of writing (and speaking) may be characterized as fluent, his expression being typical of the oratory and journalism of the day. Sometimes picturesque and striking, it is more often intricate and involved, the figures overlaid, the sense enveloped in sound.

As the *History of Sacramento* gives us insight into Dr. Morse's character, so a knowledge of his career in the city helps us to interpret his chronicle. Miss Caroline Wenzel's *Historical Note on the Life of Dr. Morse* provides this biographical background and should be read in connection with the *History*. Together they are issued by the Sacramento Book Collectors Club as the third in its published series of original documents bearing upon the history of Sacramento and California.

In reprinting the *History of Sacramento*, the publication committee has accepted the responsibility of reproducing the historical material presented by Dr. Morse without attempting to perpetuate the precise typographical form in which it first appeared. If the latter end had been sought, only facsimile reproduction would have been adequate. Following this editorial policy, certain types of revisions have been made for the purpose of clarifying the author's meaning. Typographical errors have been corrected, as have grammatical errors, which may have arisen from the haste in which the original edition was prepared for the printer. Punctuation has of necessity been modernized. Obsolete spellings, if correct at the time of writing and if they now convey the intended meaning, have been preserved, although if two spellings were used by Morse, the modem form has been preferred. Material actually added has been placed in square brackets, and a few notes have been appended when required to supply a deficiency, for the modem reader, in the text. Documents quoted in the History have been checked with original sources wherever possible and revisions or notations made accordingly.

The title, *The First History of Sacramento City*, has been fabricated for this first separate printing of the work, it having appeared in 1853 simply as the *History of Sacramento*. The appended *Historical Sketch*, 1851, taken from the city directory of that year, has been included for its own interest and for those who may quibble over its prior right to the title of first, though its brevity and sketchy nature scarcely entitle it to be called a history.

While most of the research involved in the preparation of the volume has been done in the California State Library, other institutions and individuals have made appreciable contributions. Mr. Herbert W. Erskine, grandson of Dr. Morse, has supplied information about his family and a copy of the portrait printed as an illustration in this book. To Mrs. Florence Erskine Gantner goes the credit for establishing the exact place of birth of Dr. John F. Morse. He was born in the town of Essex, Chittenden County, on the Winooski River, in the State of Vermont. This information was received too late for inclusion in the historical note. Miss Katherine Lord of Nantucket Island, Massachusetts, furnished genealogical information and cherished family letters. Mr. Carl I. Wheat has gone out of his way in search of data not readily available, as has also Dr. George D. Lyman. Several institutions have responded to requests, and we are particularly grateful to the Long Island Historical Society and the College of Medicine of New York University. In the California State Library Miss Mabel R. Gillis, State Librarian has given the fullest cooperation and has permitted the use of the original 1853 Sacramento city directory in the library's California collection. Miss Caroline Wenzel has of course made a significant contribution in the *Historical Note*, and she and other members of the California department have assisted in many ways. Several members of the Sacramento Book Collectors Club deserve special mention. Miss Margaret Preston has served as chairman of the proof-reading committee and has been assisted by Miss Evelyn Huston and Mrs. Marian Harlow. The editorial work has been done by Mr. Frugé, Mr. Harlow, and Mr. Stoddard of the publication committee. The index has been prepared by Mr. Stoddard, the decorations by Mr. Harlow. Mr. George T. Smisor, head of the printing department of Sacramento College, has supervised the printing and designing of the book and has always been helpful and tolerant.

Committee for Publication No. 3:
AUGUST FRUGÉ
NEAL HARLOW
WALTER E. STODDARD, Chairman

May, 1945

TABLE OF CONTENTS

ILLUSTRATIONS

HISTORICAL NOTE

John Fredrick Morse was born on December 25, 1815, in Essex County, Vermont, the son of Elijah Morgan Morse and Hannah Curtiss Morgan Morse. Educated to be a physician, he pursued his medical studies with that ardor and enthusiasm which characterized him in all his undertakings. After graduating from the University of the City of New York in 1844, he opened an office in Brooklyn for the practice of medicine and surgery and attained high rank among his fellows. He became identified with the order of Odd Fellows and was active in charitable and church work, being a charter member of famous old Plymouth Church which he helped establish in 1846. In 1,849, because of ill health which forced him to abandon his profession temporarily, he decided upon a voyage to California.

On February 22, 1849, at the age of thirty-three, he sailed from New York for Panama on the bark *Bogotá* with a company bound for California. His wife, Rebecca L. Canmore Morse, of Norwalk, Connecticut, whom he had married in New York on October 14, 1843, and his young daughter, Emma, did not accompany him at this time but joined him in California two years later. Upon arriving at the

Isthmus in company with other gold seekers, he experienced considerable difficulty in getting across, and when the group reached Panama they had to wait for a vessel to take them to San Francisco. Finally, on May 20, 1849, Dr. Morse obtained passage on the *Alexander von Humboldt.*

The *Humboldt*, as the vessel was popularly called, was an old ship which went around Cape Horn originally as a coal freighter and lay at Panama five months without employment until a speculative individual purchased her for a large sum and fitted her up for passengers. Captain John McArthur was in command of the vessel, while the former captain, John Clar, acted as sailing master. The fare charged was $200. Upon arriving at San Francisco the ship was condemned, but the trip proved to be historic. The passengers, many of whom subsequently became prominently identified with the history of California, formed the Humboldt Association and for many years held a reunion to commemorate their arrival.

On the voyage much hardship was endured. The passengers lived on jerked beef, hard tack, and water contained in old casks which had been soaked in whale oil. Sickness broke out and there was great suffering. While at Acapulco the ship physician was very anxious to be relieved of his obligation, and after a good deal of importuning Morse accepted the station, serving until the vessel reached San Francisco.

In a letter to his mother he wrote that one of the first things he did was to go into the steerage, which had not been cleaned since they left Panama, and "lead off in the noble function of scraper and cleaner." He commented on the fact that while "the steerage was occupied by men of excellent minds and standing . . . yet it was singular to see them daily vitiating their constitutions by breathing the most fetid air, rather than to do themselves what was obviously the duty of the stewards of the ship to attend to. The moment, however, I took my position as a sweeper, I was joined and complemented by more than were needed in either capacity." The ship arrived in San Francisco on August 3o, 1849, and apparently Morse left almost immediately with his company for the mines. Little is known of his mining experiences beyond the fact that he went to Coloma; but he was there only a few days when the group disbanded, and each one took his own course. Morse decided to settle in Sacramento and engage in the practice of medicine and surgery.

At that time Sacramento was the main seat of trade in California. It was a bustling, inflated world of commerce. Men were making fortunes in the mines, and those who remained in mercantile pursuits expected and received a corresponding remuneration for their thought, time, and trouble. Immigrants were arriving in great numbers.

The extreme prevalence of sickness, the exorbitant charges, and the lack of facilities to care for the sick were most noticeable. To meet the demand, a Sacramento firm, Priest, Lee & Co., built a hospital on the corner of K and Third streets and leased it to Drs. John F. Morse and Jacob D. B. Stillman.

The earliest printed reference to Morse's residence in Sacramento which has been noted is an advertisement which appeared in the Sacramento *Placer Times* of December 22, 1849. On that day Drs. Morse and Stillman announced to the public that their hospital was ready for the reception of patients and that a drug store would be operated in connection with the hospital. It was also announced that the doctors would continue to attend outdoor patients, an indication that both had previously practiced in the city. The notice ran until March 16, 1850, and on April 22, Dr. Stillman advertised that he had removed his office to the City Hotel.

John Fredrick Morse, M.D.
From An Oil Portrait In The Possession Of
Morse Erskine, His Grandson

It is impossible to recount the professional labors performed and gratuitous services rendered by these two men during the short time the hospital was in existence. When the big flood of January 8, 1850, occurred, the hospital was partly inundated, but the doctors remained with their patients and carried on as best they could. No assistance was given them by the newly organized City Council. The expenses were paid by a few pay-patients and outside practice. Dr. Stillman, who gives a vivid picture of the hospital at this time, wrote, "Of those who are destitute and get well, we take their notes; if they die, we take a check on Heaven."

Dr. Morse at this time was also giving generously of his services to the Sacramento Odd Fellows' Association. Shortly before he settled in Sacramento, the Odd Fellows of the city, for want of a charter, had met and formed an association for the relief of sick and distressed brothers. Dr. Morse, who had been initiated a member of Atlantic Lodge No. 50, of Brooklyn, New York; on January 20, 1845, immediately joined this group. In December of 1849 the Odd Fellows were joined by members of the Masonic order in their work of benevolence, and together they fitted up a hospital in the southeast corner of Sutter's Fort for the relief of the distressed. A board of trustees was appointed to govern the hospital, and John F. Morse was named secretary.

The board depended upon voluntary contributions and the aid of the two orders, but the burden fell upon comparatively few. Many of the subscriptions were not paid, and the trustees were greatly embarrassed by the want of general support. They were soon heavily in debt, and finally, after being sued for a large part of the amount due, they were compelled to close the hospital for a time and appeal to the public for aid. Dr. Morse worked unceasingly for the cause, helping the proprietors and managers of the Tehama Theater, Rowe's Olympic Circus, and various other organizations arrange benefits to raise money to carry on the work.

He strongly advocated the adoption of stringent measures to correct the filthy condition of the streets and promote the general health of the city. It appears that he was the first to inaugurate a system of health insurance in California, for it is stated in an announcement in the July 16, 1850, issue of the Sacramento *Transcript*, regarding the terms of the Masons' and Odd Fellows' Hospital, that a payment of $100 would entitle the subscriber to free attendance at the hospital when sick any time within a year. In October and November of 1850, when cholera ravaged the city, the hospital admitted all who applied, regardless of their financial condition. Dr. More and members of the Odd Fellows and Masonic orders were to be found giving freely of their help wherever there was sickness or death.

After Dr. Morse dissolved partnership with Dr. Stillman in April, 1850, he entered the banking and real estate business. On the twentieth of April, announcement was made that Thomas A. Warbass, William S. Heyl, and John F. Morse had formed a co-partnership under the firm name of Warbass & Co. to do business as bankers, exchange brokers, and real estate agents. We have no written word as to what induced Morse to go into commerce, but it was probably because trading at that time yielded an enormous profit. Although physicians were in great demand, their remuneration was small because of the poverty of most of their patients and the great amount of charitable work they were called upon to do. Many were compelled to take the less congenial employment of mining or business. It seemed financially wise for Dr. Morse to enter into partnership with Warbass and Heyl. But, unfortunately, soon after this partnership was formed, there was a great business depression, and in the panic that followed in the wake of the failure of Priest, Lee & Co., many business houses were forced into insolvency, including Warbass & Co., who closed their doors on August 22, 1850. This was a great blow to Dr. Morse, and in a statement issued the next day he ascribed the cause of failure to the unjust standard of value applied to gold dust. He declared that although he had only two dollars and a half cash capital remaining, he intended, just as soon as he recovered from a little bodily indisposition, to find employment in the community and pay every creditor.

Shortly after this failure, Dr. Morse, at the solicitation of his friends, became a candidate for the office of Clerk of the Supreme Court. He was defeated, however, at the election of October 7, 1850.

On October 25, he and James B. Mitchel went into business as real estate and general agents under the firm name of Morse & Mitchel. Mitchel acted as notary public and Morse as auctioneer. He retired from this partnership to accept the editorial chair of the Sacramento *Union*.

The *Union*, a newspaper begun by a group of practical printers, made its first appearance on March 19, 1851. Dr. Morse was first offered a partnership in the concern, but he declined taking any pecuniary interest, accepting instead the position of editor on a salary. In a letter to his mother dated March 29, Dr. Morse told of receiving unmerited praise as a writer, the praise, he said, being much too extravagant. The *Union* became a Whig party organ on April 29, 1851, and Morse remained as editor until May 4, 1852, when he severed his connection with the paper. A few days after his retirement the new senior editor of the *Union*, Andrew Russell, paid tribute to Morse in his editorial column. In a letter home, Morse wrote that the eulogy was really offensive, if not fulsome, and was actuated by the fact that his withdrawal from the paper had begun very seriously to affect the interests of the establishment. He left the *Union*, he said, because of an attempt to reduce his salary from $300 to $200 per month, and because his strength, never robust, was giving way under the tremendous pressure of duties he was compelled to perform.

He resumed the practice of medicine almost immediately and became associated with Drs. Thomas M. Logan and Septer Patrick. The latter withdrew from the partnership within a few months, and on July 31, 1852, Morse and Logan located in a brick building, owned by Logan, on K near Third. They announced that they were associating themselves for the purpose of practicing in the various branches of their profession and carrying on a general wholesale and retail drug business. This building was completely destroyed by the disastrous fire which occurred on the night of November 2, 1852.

In addition to the heavy financial loss sustained by Dr. Morse at this time, he suffered a severe personal one in the tragic death of his wife, Rebecca. During the fire she was removed to the steamer *Comanche*. En route to San Francisco on November 4, she gave birth to a son and died aboard the vessel a few moments after its arrival at the wharf. The son, John Francis, survived, but died in Sacramento four years later. In a letter to his mother, Morse wrote that the loss of his wife had caused him "the most poignant distress that can be realized by human beings"; and in addition, he had lost his "all pecuniarily." Property, clothes, and even coined money were totally destroyed, and this loss prevented fulfilment of a cherished plan to revisit his mother. Small wonder Dr. Morse wrote so feelingly of the early trials and tribulations of the City of Sacramento!

Shortly after the fire the following notice appeared in the local paper: "Drs. Logan and Morse may be found for the present at the Hotel de France. Enquire at the bar." On December 11, 1852, it was announced that "Dr. John F. Morse still continues to practice his profession in Sacramento, and may be found at his office over Stanford & Brothers, K Street between Second and Third," while "Dr. Logan will continue the practice of his profession at his old stand on K near the corner of Third." The following April, Morse became associated with Dr. J. S. Trowbridge for a brief period, after which he maintained his own office in Sacramento until July of 1863, when he formed a co-partnership with Dr. William R. Cluness for a short time. On September 19, 1863, he moved with his family to San Francisco to become associated with the Medical Department of the University of the Pacific. He had remarried in Sacramento on January 16, 1854, his second wife being Miss Caroline F. Loney, daughter of N. M. Loney, of Belfast, Maine. The ceremony was performed by the Rev. Joseph A. Benton, and the union proved a very happy one.

Dr. Morse was a man of great public spirit, and his name was prominently identified with the civic advancement of Sacramento almost from its beginning. He took a lively interest in every question which affected the community. He was active in political and social organizations and held many important offices, becoming widely

17

known throughout the state. With unusual fluency of speech and a rapid, impetuous delivery, he was often called upon for addresses on public occasions, and with his pen he made an even wider reputation.

He maintained a lifelong interest in the Odd Fellows and Masonic orders. With other members of the temporary Sacramento Odd Fellows' Association, he joined the first chartered Sacramento Lodge No. 2 of the I. O. O. F., which was established on January 28, 1851, and subsequently became Grand Representative to the Grand Lodge of the United States. He successfully started lodges in Germany and Switzerland in 1870, and in 1874 was delegated to instruct the Odd Fellows of the Sandwich Islands and Australia but was compelled to give up the commission because of illness. He likewise associated himself with Connecticut Lodge No. 75 (later known as Tehama Lodge No. 3) of the Masonic order, assisted in the organization of Sacramento Lodge No. 40, of which he was for a short time a member, and later joined Excelsior Lodge No. 166 at San Francisco. Herein as elsewhere he distinguished himself, becoming a Master Mason in 1852 and serving as Worshipful Master, Grand Orator, and in other responsible fraternal capacities.

Morse was one of a group who assembled on the evening of June 19, 1850, to establish a Mercantile Library Association, the purpose of which was to advance the literary and social condition of Sacramento. He was an enthusiastic supporter of the movement and was appointed on the committee to draft the constitution, also becoming corresponding secretary of the society. Citizens were encouraged to donate books and relics illustrative of the early history and development of California which could be preserved in the archives of the society and which would be invaluable "twenty years hence." Squire Pierce Dewey presented to the institution his large and valuable library consisting of about 320 volumes which he had taken pains to bring with him to California. A lecture was delivered by Morse before the Association on March 18, 1851, on the subject of the American Union, and he persuaded James Stark, the tragedian, to give a series of Shakespearean readings as a benefit. The Association was one of the earliest literary and historical organizations of its kind in the state.

During the years 1852 to 1855, while Dr. Morse's office was located over Stanford & Brothers' store, he became a close friend of Theodore Judah, Leland Stanford, and other future railroad officials and later took great interest in the construction of the Sacramento Valley and Central Pacific railroads. The statement has been repeatedly made that he was one of a party of four to take the first railroad ride in California on the Sacramento Valley line, but his name has in this connection apparently been confused with that of George W. Mowe.

According to the Articles of Association filed in the office of the Secretary of State of California on June 28, 1861, Morse was one of the original stockholders of the Central Pacific Railroad, having held five shares. In 1862 he became a member of its board of directors. He was active in selling stock, and was one of the speakers at an informal meeting of forty or fifty of the "solid men" of Sacramento who gathered together on the evening of October 23, 1862, at the rooms of the Central Pacific Railroad Company to consider measures to encourage subscriptions to the capital stock of the company. He had the honor of representing the Society of California Pioneers at the ceremony of breaking ground for the railroad in Sacramento on January 8, 1863, and was one of the speakers on this memorable occasion.

The Sacramento Medico-Chirurgical Academy was founded on May 8, 1850, and Dr. Morse was elected first vice-president and orator. The objects of the Academy were the cultivation of science, the promotion of honor, dignity, and interest of the profession, and the separation of the regular from the irregular practitioners. The local newspaper stated that it was believed to be the first association for scientific purposes in the state, and it announced that on May 22 Dr. Morse would deliver the first lecture on scientific and secular subjects in California. In November, Morse was appointed on a committee to encourage citizens to adopt sanitary measures to prevent the spread of cholera, then rampant in Sacramento. After a few years the Academy ceased to exist.

On the evening of April 30, 1855, a group of the more prominent members of the medical profession of Sacramento met and organized an association under the name of the Sacramento Medical Society. The society was formed for the purpose of protecting regular practitioners and the public from the innovations and malpractice of uneducated pretenders. Dr. Morse was elected second vice-president. This society antedated by thirteen years the Sacramento Society for Medical Improvement, which was organized on March 17, 1868, and is still in existence.

When members of the medical profession throughout the state of California met in Sacramento on March 12, 1856, for the purpose of forming the Medical Society of the State of California, Dr. Morse was chosen temporary chairman of the convention, elected as one of the seven censors, and appointed a member of the standing committees on medical education and publication. There was at the time no journal devoted to the interests of the medical profession being published in California, so a committee was appointed to arrange some practical plan to issue such a magazine. It was finally decided that Dr. Morse, who had been making preliminary arrangements to publish an independent medical journal on his own responsibility, should undertake the task. Dr. Logan, as chairman of the committee, then recommended Dr. Morse as publisher, and spoke most favorably of him as "one of the pioneers of our noble profession who has identified himself with every work of progress in this community, moral, social, or medical—a gentleman thoroughly drilled, by long experience, in the tactics of editorial discipline, and whose devotion to his science has been manifested by the active part he has taken in the formation and development of the present auspicious phases in medical affairs." The members of the society were pledged to support and sustain the publication of the journal. Thus it was that

John F. Morse had the honor of being the editor and proprietor of *The California State Medical Journal*, the first number of which was published in July, 1856.

The *Journal* was soundly built and meritorious in every respect, containing scientific papers and local items of medical importance. Quarterly publication was continued until April, 1857, when the editor was forced to discontinue for lack of financial support. It was a brave endeavor on Morse's part, inspired by his earnest desire for the establishment of a respectable medical journal in the state. It was with regret that he was forced to abandon the idea, but it was a relief to be free of the vast amount of labor, anxiety, and pecuniary loss suffered by him during his time of editorship. Many years later the *California State Journal of Medicine* appeared as the subsidized organ of the state society. In the sixties Morse served as temporary editor of the *Pacific Medical and Surgical Journal*, succeeding Dr. Victor J. Fourgeaud in October, 1864, and serving in this capacity until April, 1865.

Morse was associated with his friend James Lloyd Lafayette Warren in the establishment of the *California Farmer and Journal of Useful Sciences*, the first agricultural paper on the Pacific Coast. The first number appeared on January 5, 1854, and Morse served as editor for a short period, terminating his connection after the publication of the seventh issue, on February 16, 1854. At this time the journal was published in San Francisco but the editor's office was in Sacramento. Warren, in an editorial dated April 20, stated that "the engagements of the Doctor in his profession, and in the issue of the *History of the Valley of Sacramento*, together with other engagements, made it necessary that we should assume entire control of the *Farmer* . . . and we cannot refrain from an earnest wish that our former associate may find much pleasure in the reflection that he has been instrumental in thus sending forth upon the ocean of literature an Agricultural Journal upon the shores of the Pacific.... We regret losing the presence and associate labors of our friend; but wish him abundant success in the profession which he so much honors. We hope he will be sustained and prosper in the *History of the Valley.* . ."

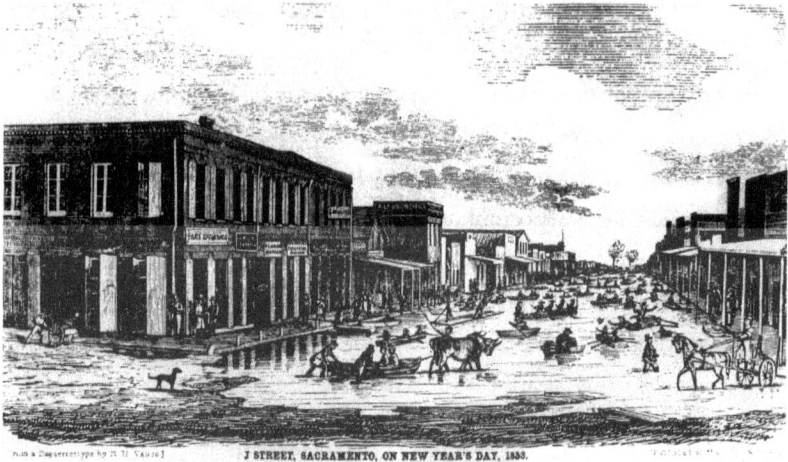

J STREET, SACRAMENTO, ON NEW YEAR'S DAY, 1853.

FLOOD OF THE WINTER OF 1852-1853
FROM A LETTERSHEET UPON WHICH DR. MORSE
PENNED A LETTER TO HIS MOTHER. THE LETTER-SHEET
IS NOW IN THE CALIFORNIA STATE LIBRARY

Always intensely interested in agriculture, Dr. Morse was one of the best informed men in the state on the subject. His address on agriculture delivered at the American Theater in Sacramento on October 7, 1852, to a large group of citizens attending an agricultural fair sponsored by Warren & Co. was published in full in the newspapers and widely acclaimed. He proposed in this address that a convention be called to organize a state agricultural society. Such a meeting was held in January, 1854, and resulted in the formation of the State Agricultural Society, incorporated by the legislature on May 13, 1854. This society is still active in promoting the annual California State Fair, one of America's leading agricultural expositions. Morse received a silver goblet in appreciation of his efforts. He became a life member and was frequently called upon to give the annual oration.

Dr. Morse was a member of the Whig State Central
Committee and on February 27, 1852, was elected vice-chairman and
took an active part in the meeting held in Sacramento on June 8.
Governor Leland Stanford appointed him to serve as a trustee of the
California State Library in 1862, and he was duly elected to this office
by the California legislature in joint convention on January 27, 1863.
He served in this position until the latter part of the following year. In
1864 his name was suggested as a member of the commission to
manage Yosemite Valley. When the California Prison Commission was
organized November 27, 1865, Governor Frederick F. Low was
elected president and John F. Morse vice-president. However, the
latter served as acting president and was subsequently elected president
for the year 1867. He was so deeply interested in the commission that
he became a life member, giving freely of his time and money to the
cause.

On April 2, 1855, he was elected school trustee for the first
ward. In the early days the membership in the Volunteer Fire
Department included the most prominent citizens, merchants, lawyers,
doctors, and statesmen, and we find Morse's name listed in the
Sacramento directory of 1855 as one of the physicians who had
volunteered their services. He was an active member of the
Sacramento Society of California Pioneers, serving as director in 1854-
1855, vice-president 1855-1856, and president in 1857-1859. He
contributed twenty-five valuable books for the purpose of forming the
nucleus of a library for the society.

At San Francisco in the fall of 1863, Dr. Morse assumed his
duties as Professor of Medicine in the Medical Department of the
University of the Pacific. The university, later the College of the
Pacific, was located at San Jose but about 1858 chartered a medical
department in San Francisco, the first medical school in California.
The chair of the Theory and Practice of Medicine had been made
vacant by several important changes in the department following the
death of Dr. Elias S. Cooper, founder of the school. The *San Francisco*

Medical Press, in commenting on Morse's appointment, stated, "The school has secured for itself a thorough and accurate medical scholar, a ready and easy lecturer, and what is most needed by the student, a prompt and assiduous teacher." He remained with the University of the Pacific until October, 1864, when he joined the original faculty of Toland Medical College, a school which was later to be absorbed by the Medical Department of the University of California. He remained as Professor of Theory and Practice of Medicine and Clinical Medicine and Diagnosis until 1870, and in 1874 affiliated, as Professor Emeritus in Medicine, with the newly reorganized medical faculty of the University of the Pacific, a forerunner of Stanford University Medical School.

In addition to his duties as an instructor, Morse had also been carrying on a large and successful private practice, sharing his office for a time with Dr. James P. Whitney (1864-1865) and later with Dr. J. R. Prevost (1872-1873). His active career of usefulness both to his profession and to society continued until ill health, in the form of the dread tuberculosis, forced him into retirement. The greater portion of the last five years of his life was spent in travel. Late in 1874 he took passage for Australia, hoping the sea voyage would recuperate his health, but at Honolulu his condition caused him to abandon the trip and return by the next steamer. He reached home a few days before his death, which occurred in San Francisco on December 30, 1874, three days past his fifty-ninth birthday.

Dr. Morse was survived by his widow, Caroline, who died in San Francisco on September 5, 1907, at the age of 79 years, and one son and four daughters. His son, Dr. John F. Morse, Jr., the brilliant surgeon, practiced in San Francisco until his untimely death on August 21, 1898. Emma, the eldest daughter, married Dr. Joseph Remy Prevost, dying in San Francisco on June 2, 1876, at the early age of twenty-eight years. Nellie, who married Francis W. Shingleberger, also died in San Francisco in January, 1881. Caroline, the widow of William Wilson Erskine, passed away in San Francisco on April 29, 1944, aged eighty years, and Henrietta, the widow of Morris W. Rehfisch, is still living in Berkeley. The descendants of these children are prominently identified with the state's history and a number of them now serve in the armed forces of the country.

The funeral of Dr. Morse took place on the same day as that of another famous early California physician, Dr. Victor J. Fourgeaud. It was one of the largest ever seen in San Francisco, and few men in California have left a larger circle of warmly attached personal friends. He was universally esteemed; his wide interests and sympathetic nature coupled with a gracious personality made him popular not only in medical and fraternal circles but in all other walks of life. As recently as April, 1934, his memory was honored by services held at Mount Olivet Cemetery, San Mateo County, commemorating the transfer of a statue of Dr. Morse which had been in the old Odd Fellows' Cemetery in San Francisco since 1879. The monument, the work of Marion Wells, had been erected largely through the contributions of school children. Hundreds attended the Odd Fellows' ceremonies, and among the speakers was a grandson, Herbert E. Erskine.

Dr. Morse was truly one of California's foremost pioneers. He was an active participant in the stirring events which characterized Sacramento's early days. It was typical of the man that he should realize it was a matter of importance as well as of thrilling interest to rescue the history of his time from fading memory and put it in some enduring and acceptable form for future contemplation. To him goes the credit of writing *The First History of Sacramento City*, the earliest consequential record of the city to appear in print.

CAROLINE WENZEL.

California Room
California State Library, Sacramento

AUTHOR'S NOTE TO THE PUBLISHER

SAMUEL COLVILLE, ESQ.:

My Dear Sir: In publishing to the world the following sketch of our city, you must assume the responsibility of the many imperfections with which it is marked; for although you have most zealously engaged in the work of collecting the principal data from which the sketch is constructed, yet you have given so little time for the completion of the task assigned to me that I should be most unwilling to have it presented as a well digested and carefully written history. Many references to individuals and events have been necessarily omitted, which we will endeavor to make in an enlarged edition.

For the many typographical errors haste must be the apologist.

Yours truly,

John F. Morse.

Sacramento, October 10th, 1853

HISTORY OF SACRAMENTO

The city of Sacramento is situated on the eastern bank of the Sacramento River immediately below the confluence of the American Fork. The first survey of the town was made during the month of December, 1848, by Capt. William H. Warner of United States Army.

Prior, however, to commencing our historical sketch of the city, we will indulge in a cursory glance at some of the interesting incidents and influences which led to the design of locating a town upon the bank of the Sacramento and which resulted in the permanent selection of the site now occupied. Up to 1844 the fort of Capt. John A. Sutter constituted the principal trading post in Upper California. It was the only prominent and absorbing point of interest in this section of the then Mexican territory. It had acquired a renown almost unequalled from the warm and prodigal hospitality of its bold and venerated founder. It had become identified with every sketch of exploration that was made of California, was the very center and birthplace of that enterprise which superinduced the great gold discovery of January, 1848, and achieved a general reputation in the history of the world which will make it an eternal disgrace to the government that has allowed it to fall into rapid and disgusting dilapidation, a dilapidation not alone resulting from the mutations of time but from the most degrading uses to which it could have been appropriated— that of hen-roosts and hog-pens.

In the year 1844 an effort was made under the patronage of Capt. Sutter and others located at the fort to lay out and build up a town at a point three miles below this, now called Sutter. A survey was made and a village commenced. The first house was erected by Capt. Sutter, the second by one Hadel, and the third by a Mr. Zins The last was a brick building and, we are informed, the first that was put up in California. This place flourished, which had been named Sutterville in honor of its projector, without any other rival than Sutter's Fort until about the time of the gold discovery, prior to which it was selected as a garrison for a couple of companies of U. S. soldiers under the command of Major Kingsbury.

At the time, and shortly after the discovery of gold, there were quite a number of stores located at the fort. This indeed seems to have been the principal business center if we may judge from the merchants engaged in business at that point. The first store in existence (we are informed by Mr. Kemble of the *Alta California*) on the discovery of gold was the store of C. C. Smith & Co., Samuel Brannan being the Co. This was started a few months prior to the opening of the mines, and across its counter were made the first exchanges of American goods for California gold. Brannan subsequently became the sole owner of the store. His store was kept in the Old adobe building afterwards used as a hospital. Hensley & Reading had their store in the walls of the fort, and James King of William was their clerk. Besides these were Messrs. Murray & Lappeas, Pickett & Co., Priest, Lee & Co., Sadgett & Co., and other merchants engaged in the mercantile business at that place.

On the 28th of April, '49, the Placer Times was commenced at the fort. It was then issued as a weekly upon foolscap, and E.C. Kemble was the editor, typist, printer, and publisher of this pioneer paper of the valley.

The discovery of gold gave a new impulse to matters, and the poor ill-fated town of Sutterville met with a powerful antagonist in the newly laid out City of Sacramento at the point described in the beginning. Shortly after the survey of Sacramento had been made, George McDougal procured a lease from Capt. Sutter of the ferry privilege at a point below the entrance to Sutter Lake. This was followed by his bringing up a storeship and locating it by the bank of the river nearly opposite I Street. Then he opened a store with a large stock of goods, in company with Judge Blackburn of Santa Cruz.

He had not been long engaged in this enterprise when the arrival of the son of Capt. Sutter effected an important change in the destiny of the new city. After he came to the country, the old captain made a conveyance of his entire interest in the city to him.[1] On the 30th of December, about two months subsequent to the arrival of

---

[1] John A. Sutter, Jr. arrived at San Francisco on September 14, 1848, and it was he who employed William H. Warner to lay out the town. His father transferred the property to his name on October 14, 1848. This phase of the history of the city is treated in detail in John Sutter, Jr., *Statement Regarding Early California Experiences, Edited, with a Biography, by Allan R. Ottley.* Sacramento Book Collectors Club, 1943.

John A. Sutter, Jr., Judge Burnett (since governor) was employed as the lawyer of the young man and assisted him in the management of his newly acquired interests.

Immediately afterwards, a question arose between George McDougal and Sutter, Jr., in respect to the prerogatives of his lease. McDougal claimed that the lease conveyed to him the exclusive right to the use of four hundred yards of the river bank from the slough down. The lease, however, had not been so written as to sustain him in his claim, and he was consequently defeated. This made him so disaffected towards the place that he determined to extinguish the prospects of the new city and accordingly moved to Sutterville. After he had transported all his goods to this point, John McDougal was given charge of the interests of this firm, his brother George having gone to the Atlantic States. The manager, John McDougal, then came out with immense placards nearly equal to the recent express train elephant cards of McNulty & Co., declaring that the firm over which he presided had determined to take the lead in competition and, accordingly, that they would sell goods at "cost and freight" with a verbal assurance that if they could not obtain patronage at that rate, they would sell at the primary cost of their merchandise. This card, when posted at the fort, produced a consternation among the traders at that point and resulted in a combination of purchasers that insidiously relieved the firm of McDougal & Co. of the means of sustaining an attractive opposition. A variety of goods once broken into at that date could not be restored, and consequently Sutterville had no recourse in her emulation of cityship except a priority of claim and certain topographical superiorities, consisting of an Immense slough of stagnant waters bounded in front by a narrow and inadequate bank and in the rear by a ridge of land just high enough to catch the fullest benefit of a concentrated and irresistible miasm. Thus did Sutterville by a most perverted folly strive to suffocate its infant rival, Sacramento.

Prior to the removal of McDougal's store, Hensley & Reading had erected the first frame building in Sacramento sometime in the month of January, '49, on the corner of I and Front streets. Soon after this a Mr. Ingersoll put up a kind of tent and frame house between J and K on Front, and Mr. Stewart a canvas house on the bank of the river between I and J which was opened as a sort of tavern. In February following, Samuel Brannan built a frame store on the corner of J and Front which was soon succeeded by the new frame store of Priest, Lee & Co., on the corner of J and Second streets and, in close succession, two very unique log houses were erected by Mr. Gillespie and Dr. Carpenter respectively.

This rapid advancement of the new town did not take place until Samuel Brannan, Judge Burnett, and Priest, Lee & Co. had accomplished a little speculating *coup d' état* which put them in possession of some five hundred of the choice lots in the embryo city. The way in which this was effected, we are informed, was this: The above parties, perceiving the struggles of Sutterville against Sacramento, found it very convenient to manifest a strong preference for the latter place. The Suttervillians quickly saw what must be the result of so much enterprise contending against them and accordingly approached their opponents with a proposition to buy them off in favor of Sutterville. They offered the Sacramento parties mentioned some eighty lots if they would abandon Sacramento and move to Sutterville. The proposition, having been taken under advisement, became a powerful element of speculation with the unsophisticated and plastic John A. Sutter, Jr., who was at that time the undisputed owner of the Sacramento site. With this argument they had no difficulty in convincing Mr. Sutter, Jr., that there was but one way of exterminating his great rival and that was by deeding to the aforesaid parties such a number of lots as would make it totally improbable for him to be out-bid in the contest. The manifest disinterestedness of the negotiators satisfied Mr. Sutter, Jr., that the proposition was not only scrupulously correct but that it was infinitely better to possess one-fifth than the whole of such valuable property. Consequently he made a conveyance of five hundred lots to these gentlemen and thus confirmed them in their conscientious devotion to a town which by a thousand declarations never had [been] and never could be flooded. Fortunately for those interested in representing the town as entirely exempt from inundation, the winter of '47 and '48 was sufficiently dry to give plausibility to the story.

From all the evidence we can gather, the number of inhabitants at the fort and in Sacramento did not exceed one hundred and fifty individuals up to the 1st of April, '49.

In the fall of '48 an election was held at the fort for first and second alcaldes, which resulted in the selection of Frank Bates and John S. Fowler. Fowler resigned in the spring following, and H. A. Schoolcraft was elected to fill the vacancy. In the spring of '49 Messrs. Brannan, Snyder, Slater, Hensley, King, Cheever, McCoover, McDougal, Barton Lee, Fette, Dr. Carpenter, Southard, and Fowler, were elected a Board of Commissioners to frame a code of laws for the district.[2]

Pursuant to the wish of this legislating committee, the people convened together under a broad spreading oak at the foot of I Street. The report which was then officially submitted, and which was duly accepted by the sovereigns assembled, provided the following officers of a jurisdiction extending from the Coast Range to the Sierra Nevada and throughout the length of the Sacramento Valley, to wit: one alcalde and a sheriff.

H. A. Schoolcraft was then elected Alcalde, and A. M. Turner, Sheriff. This constituted the judiciary of northern California up to the time of those changes that took place in very rapid succession after the immigration of '49, began to concentrate at Sacramento.

Through the months of February, March, April, and May of '49, there was a regular and unbroken improvement of the town, which demonstrated the operation of influences that have since confirmed Sacramento as the second city in our Pacific possessions. Thus did the *Embarcadero*[3] triumph over its malicious neighbor, Sutterville, a town which had been unwisely located upon a slough of

---

[2] The members of this body "with full powers to enact laws for the government of the city and district" were Samuel Brannan, Peter Slater, James King of William, Henry Cheever, M.M. McCarver, John McDougal, Barton Lee, William Pettit, William M. Carpenter, Charles G. Southard, and John S. Fowler. (Sacramento *Placer Times*, May 5, 1849, p. 1, col. 1) The two additional men listed by Morse, Jacob Rink Snyder and Samuel Hensley, were not candidates.

[3] Sacramento was laid out along the east bank of the Sacramento River at what was known as Sutter's *Embarcadero, the landing place for the freight and passengers going to Sutter's Fort.*

stagnant waters and which became to the speculators in the scheme a slough of despondency.

From the commencement of the town of Sacramento until the first of June, the progress of improvement was comparatively gradual. The immigration was limited in contrast with what followed, and yet it evolved a most interesting period in the history of the Levee City. Everything wore such an anomalous appearance; there was no law, system, nor consistency, and yet there was no absolute disorder or discord. The whole fabric of society was little less than chaos; and still there were a oneness and harmony in its movements which can scarcely be paralleled in the annals of the world. The general admixture was most perfect and inimitable, although the elements of which it was composed were as diverse as nations, nature, or caprice could make them. There was no moral restraint, and yet for months there never was a community more perfectly exempt from violence and immorality. There was really no government, no acknowledged standard to regulate the concessions and mutual forbearances of a common intercourse and neighborhood relations, and yet no person was ungoverned, and the spirit of accommodation sat in radiance upon all the transactions of a mass thus singularly blended.

The old pioneers and newly arrived adventurers constituted at that time but a small and insignificant community, and whilst they were fully impressed with an idea of the profusion of riches that surrounded them, they had not as yet a conception of the convulsive throes and conflicts of passion to which a pursuit of California gold must inevitably lead. They had given themselves up to such a conviction of independence that they could not anticipate an interruption of their advantages; and then there was such a glorious and intoxicating

37

equality, such a total dependence upon an innate chivalry, such a uniformity of rights and utter dethronement of the uncomfortable distinctions of society, that any man could reign as peasant, nabob, or king without a fear of incurring odium or the possibility of giving offense.

But in order that a more accurate idea of the character of the people may be conveyed, we will collect and describe some of the incidents and scenes marking the interval in progress.

Some time in April of '49 a party of six gentlemen, landing at Sacramento, gave a most interesting entertainment to Capt. Sutter upon the bank of the river just above the outlet of Sutter Lake The visitors consisted of Lieuts. May, Hammersly, Elliott, Fauntleroy, and Peachy, and Corse of the U. S. Navy. The first three individuals had been previously engaged by the Exploring Expedition under Lieut. Wilkes in an exploration of the Sacramento River a considerable distance above this point. During the previous reconnoissance of the river they visited the old pioneer of the country at his fort, and the grateful recollection of his exhaustless kindness to them at that early date made them do their utmost to manifest their esteem of so excellent a man. Immediately after landing they hastened to the fort where they enjoyed one of those warm and thrilling greetings which results from an unexpected meeting of congenial spirits after a long absence. Their first mission to the fort was to assure themselves of the old captain's recognition and to invite him to a dinner with them upon the following day. The appointed time brought the dinner hour and their guest, and with minds attuned for an electric enjoyment of a most novel and interesting scene, they sat down to the best repast that could be prepared at that time in the new city. The dishes provided consisted of boiled ham, roast beef, and a bountiful supply of hard bread. After the gastric economy had been thoroughly feasted upon these, the more substantial and necessary elements of physical life, then, sailor like, champagne, at a cost of $16 per bottle, was produced as copiously as if it had been bottled from the river that flowed by their side. It is, indeed, intimated that so bountiful were the libations of the feast that an adjournment of the rising was taken until the next morning by silent consent, and that it was utterly impossible for any individual present to count the number of bottles uncorked for the occasion. This, however, is probably nothing more than a slanderous appendix to the book of incidents and interests which might have been written upon the entertainment.

We are told by Mr. Cornwall, who was one of the firm of Priest, Lee & Co., that trading at that time yielded an enormous profit. Fifty per cent, he says, would have covered the expenses incurred in bringing their goods from San Francisco to Sacramento, and yet their sales would average two hundred per cent over the San Francisco cost of merchandise. And whilst such profits were cheerfully granted, there was still another ultimate and powerful profit realized from the gold dust which, although the main currency of the country, had not as yet been adjusted to any fixed standard. The scale of valuation ranged from $8 to $16 per ounce from the discovery of gold up to the 1st of June, '49. Clerks in stores received salaries from three to five hundred dollars per month, and few could be retained for any price. A brisk trade was commencing between the Sacramentans and the miners. A constant change of purchasers was taking place, and yet such was the marvelous spirit of honesty which prevailed that neither goods nor gold dust were watched with the least care or consideration. Miners coming to town, freighted with bags of the valuable ore, stowed away their treasure as indifferently as they did their hats and boots and lay down at night to slumbers that could only be broken by the waking beams of fair Aurora.

On the 5th of May, '49, Mr. Kemble informs us[4] that Sacramento was being built up with great rapidity. He says there were at that time about thirty buildings occupied by stores. A bark of 300 and a brig of 200 tons burthen were moored along the bank of the river, and also the bark *Whiton*, which had been commanded by Capt. R. Gelsten, 72 hours from San Francisco and 140 days from New York. The trip of this vessel up the river was regarded an extraordinary quick one—small boats and launches usually requiring five and ten days to make the ascent of the Sacramento.

It will be remembered that the interval which we are contemplating includes the period of interruption given to immigration from the desertion of sailors and working hands on the steamers. The *California* and *Oregon* of the P. M. S. S. Co.,[5] after landing their first cargoes of passengers, were compelled, from this cause, to lie by at San Francisco. But, as we have mentioned, in the latter part of May immigration began to come in from sailing vessels, and in June every avenue of immigration was opened, and thousands upon thousands began to concentrate at this point preparatory to their mining adventures. Sacramento then began her career as a most important trading center. It was the grand starting point to every new coming gold seeker whose predilections led him to the northern mines; and it was but a very small proportion of the miners of '49 that gave a preference to the "southern diggings." The forks of the American, Bear, Yuba, and Feather rivers, with their various branches, constituted the great aggregate of attraction and made Sacramento the

---

[4] In the Sacramento *Placer Times,* May 5, 1849, p. 2, col. 1-2

[5] The Pacific Mail Steamship Company

peculiar town for the purchase of gold digging implements and provisions. In June everything in and about the city indicated an overwhelming business, conducted without a particle of method and in such utter confusion and recklessness of manner as to make it impossible for a man to construct calculations that embraced more than the contingencies of a single day. From this time the trade or transportation of the river, from San Francisco, became an enormous source of profit, and every craft that could be procured was crowded into the business. Schooners from 5o to 15o tons would command any price from 200 to 3,000 per cent upon cost, whilst the finest merchant ships that entered the bay at San Francisco could hardly beget a sufficient interest to preserve them from destruction. The price of passage from San Francisco to Sacramento at that time was variously ranging from $16 to $25. Freight ranged proportionately high.

On the 26th of June, Sacramento numbered one hundred houses. The large City Hotel, which became a house of great distinction, was in process of erection by Samuel Brannan & Co. This house was located on Front between I and J streets next to the site of the present Hotel Française. The building, which was previously framed for a saw and grist mill by Capt. John A. Sutter, was 35 x 55 and three stories high.

It is reported to have cost $100,000, and it was subsequently leased to Messrs. Fowler & Fry at a monthly rent of $5,000. The town was now beginning to attract attention as the prospective second city, and in the minds of a few visionaries the city of California. Trade was accumulating with a rapidity that could not be understood. Every material that could be used in the building of tents, houses, and stores became of immense value, commanding almost instant sale at any price which might be suggested by the unscrupulous spirit of specu-lation that began to manifest itself. Muslins, calicoes, canvas, old sails, brush, logs, boards, iron, zinc, tin, adobes, and boxes were infinitely more glittering and beautiful as building appliances than the unpolished gold scales which were lavishly given in exchange for them. Immigrants were making their entrance in great numbers, and the passenger and freight schooners that plied upon the river were realizing revenues that would have astounded a Cunard or Collins, in their gigantic estimates of enterprise and proceeds. As was common at that early day, public gambling became one of the leading and absorbing features of our city's progress and greatness. Gaming, in the early history of California towns, was the first and only business, the votaries of which engaged in an emulation of architectural comforts, capacity, and adornments. When merchants and bankers, corporations and churchmen, would not hazard a dollar in the development of an architectural beauty or comfort, gamesters were vying with each other in the erection of magnificent saloons at an expense that would startle credulity and pervade the soul of a reflecting man with a shudder.

Long ere San Francisco could boast of a store or hotel that was even decently related to the immense commerce which she concentrated, her public plaza was margined by these saloons, which, in capacity, in bright and glaring illuminations, in gaudy and expensive furniture, would eclipse almost any of the concert, ball, or literary halls in the Atlantic States. And what was true of San Francisco in this particular was true of Sacramento and every other town which achieved any importance in the year of '43.

The first place of public gaming in this city was situated in J Street between Second and Third, the present site of the Diana. A few poles stuck in the ground and covered with a windsail constituted this first gaming rendezvous and bore the very appropriate name of

Stinking Tent. [6] It was kept by James Lee. The principal if not exclusive game was monte. About the 1st of July a sort of shantee was erected by Locke & Waterhouse on the south side of J between First and Second streets, covered with clapboards on the sides and a muslin roof. In the latter part of this month Z. Hubbard put up the long remembered Round Tent, first on J between Front and Second streets and afterwards on Front between I and J. This tent covered an area of about fifty feet diameter and was the principal gambling center at the time. Music and a decorated bar and obscene pictures were the great attractions that lined this whirlpool of fortune and coerced into the vortex of penury and disgrace many an American who had come to California without his morals or the decencies which he was taught at home. Every species of gaming was here presented in its most winning aspect. From the A. B. C. and the sweat cloth to faro and monte there was nothing but games of hazard, at which the representatives of all nations and all avocations, not excepting some of the consecrated expounders of Gospel precepts, were present to witness and participate in the general compound of vice. Coin was at that time too scarce to be used as a betting currency by both parties at a game, and, consequently, gold dust in bags became the pledge of chance. Those who indulged in betting deposited their bags of gold dust with the players and drew from the gamesters the amount of coin necessary to play with convenience as a sort of loan—a loan which seldom failed to work the speedy ruin of the parties negotiating the favor.

---

[6] The windsail was a funnel of sail cloth let down a ship's hatchway to force fresh air below deck. This previous association, coupled woth the strong odor of the canvas itself, particulary when wet, was probably responsible for the name of the establishment.

43

It would be impossible to describe the scenes which this tent, the lineal descendant of its "stinking" ancestor, presented. Nothing but the genius of a Hogarth could have delineated its detail, and nothing short of the sketching powers of a Cruikshank could have exhibited its naked, unmasked depravity.

The toilers of the country, including traders, mechanics, miners, and speculators, lawyers, doctors, and ministers, concentrated at this gambling focus like flying insects around a lighted candle at night; and like such insects seldom left the delusive glare until scorched and consumed by the watch fires of destruction.

The gaming at this time was of a most herculean grade so far as boldness and amounts hazarded were concerned. Every saloon, every table devoted to betting contingencies was literally crowded and sometimes so completely overwhelmed as to make it physically dangerous to be even a spectator of the scenes. Not one man in ten, if one in twenty, either by his absence or denunciation, condemned the universal mania for gambling which swept the country. Two ministers of the Gospel, very soon after these saloons were opened, could be seen, one of them most piously engaged in dealing monte, and the other, with less concentration, running about trying his luck now at faro, now at monte, anon at poker, and next, perhaps, at vantoon[7] or at the legitimately named sweat cloth.

Poker was a great game; although it was not so popular as a public betting medium, yet it was the test scene of the mightiest hazards then made. While the necessitous small fry among the old votaries of the vice and the mincing minnies who for the first time

---

[7] The card game of vingt-et-un or twenty-one.

44

struck out upon the shoally ocean were risking their little upon the "Eagle Bird"[8] by chance, the bold and monied speculators in gambling would almost always be found at the table where each man became a player at the great western game of poker. At this game during that period immense fortunes were thrown into the scale of chance and circulated amidst a sphere of strangers as freely as though they were but fruits for refreshment. Ten thousand dollars would be lost or won in a few fleeting hours without exciting the least apparent inconvenience to the party at play. It was common in those days to see poker played in which the *ante* (as it was termed) was a hundred dollars each, and from $1,000 to $2,500 bet on the best hands.

Rapidly in the progress of the city did these places accumulate. The most popular place for a short time after the wane of the Round Tent was the Gem, a frame building erected on the corner of Second and J by McKinney and others and kept by Jos. McKinney, who afterwards became the sheriff of the county. Following the Gem were the Humboldt, Mansion, Empire, Lee's Exchange, Diana, and an almost innumerable range of quarter-ounce establishments, speedily built up and opened with some kind of musical attraction and rum-drinking facilities.

Such was the popularity of gambling at that period that the leaders in the craft were men of immense influence and for a short time nearly controlled the destinies of the new city. Hundreds and thousands of men who had been reared to regard gambling as a stain upon the character of a man, who had left their homes by means of borrowed money, and left behind them women and children to toil for

---

[8] **One of the figures on a roulette wheel.**

45

their subsistence until die golden dreams of California should be realized—hundreds and thousands of such men could be seen crowding these miserable haunts of ruin and gambling away the first hundred or thousand dollars which they made in the country.

Many men who had at once gone to the mines after arriving in this place and who, in a few months, had succeeded in getting a few hundred dollars together and had returned to die city with the manly and noble intention of remitting to dependent wives, unprotected children, or, peradventure, to indigent and helpless parents, have stepped into these haunts of peril for a moment in the evening and never returned until their money, character, good intentions, and peace of mind had been lost at the polluting altar of unproductive and self destroying avocations.

But whilst gambling was given a temporary ascendency in the incipient career of our city in consequence of the free and easy habits of its votaries and the greater attractions with which vice and error always surround themselves, there was an antagonism in embryo which has since effected an almost total revolution in public sentiment.

In April, '49, we are told by Rev. Mr. Benton, the Rev. Mr. Woodbridge of Benicia preached the first sermon in Sacramento. This, however, was but a single effort, and months passed away before any decided and effective steps were taken to establish regular religious services. In June, we believe, Dr. Deal, who was engaged in the practice of medicine and general trading, commenced a somewhat systematic effort to establish regular Sabbath preaching.

Following these efforts were still more effective ones through the arrival and noble ministrations of one of the most zealous and worthy of California's ministry. We mean the Rev. Mr. Benton, who

46

commenced his labors in this city during the early part of July, '49. His course from the first, so far as a close observation from that period until now affords means for judging, was most consistent. He was essentially a minister of the Gospel—a seven days' advocate of the Christian religion. He purchased no lots on speculation, never attended the Horse Market [9] as a surveyor of pecuniary chances, did not deal in corned beef, pork, sauerkraut, nor mining implements, and we believe never dealt monte, played poker, nor bet at faro. And yet with all these eccentric exceptions from the prevailing entertainments (for so they were not unfrequently called) he was around, among, and one of the people. His brow was seldom clouded with an intolerant observation, and his tongue was not too bitterly charged with denunciation. Hence he wielded a moral influence outside of the immediate sphere of church worshippers. He made himself at that time the most adroit exponent of the only species of Christian practice which could or would command a tolerable support. But that he may be still better represented, we will quote from one of his historical sermons, dating from his first Sabbath.

"On the following Sabbath the speaker preached to one hundred or so people met under the trees near the corner of Fourth and K, where were several wagons, ox yokes, and chains. A few chairs were brought. There were three ladies in from the fort, who occupied

---

[9] A popular trading center in the city where goods of every description were auctioned; but as the chief trade was livestock —horses and mules for the mines, beef cattle for the city butchers — and of a highly speculative nature, it became universally known as the Horse Market. A common meeting place, it was characterized by an early day resident and the "Commercial Exchange, Board of Trade and Chamber of Commerce all in one." (*Luzena Stanley Wilson, 49er.* Mills College, CA., Eucalytus Press, 1937, p.13) It was situated on K Street beyond 5th.

die chairs. The speaker had his seat and took his place on one of the wagons. The choir sat on the wagon tongue. The air was delightful, and die services passed off quite to the satisfaction of die audience. There was no observance of die day except by those who thus withdrew from the noise and business of a bustling little city that might then have been put in three blocks. Sunday was almost a forgotten day; and many have not recovered their memory since; they never could remember names, and the days trouble them more than any other things with names.

"After spending two Sabbaths thus, the speaker was absent the two following ones and preached on one of them on the Mokelumne, near where Mokelumne Hill now stands, to a company of miners. He slept on the ground in the open air during this tour without inconvenience. He was gone less than two weeks, and during them the city doubled in size. The emigration came in from the Plains, and there was no point to stop at short of this. Soon after, the stock market took its rise—the emigrants having camped on each side of the road just out of town. From the middle of August onward there was no such thing as keeping pace with the growth of the town in population, tents, and buildings. They sprang up like magic, scores in a day.

"On the second Sabbath in August, the speaker and Rev. Mr. Cook, a Baptist preacher just come, preached under a shelter in Third Street. There are some now in Sacramento who can remember that occasion. Before another Sabbath he was prostrated by sickness and was unable to preach again till October. The meetings went on, however, in care of Dr. Deal and Mr. Cook. He was able to be about part of the time; and about the middle of September this church organization was effected. Soon after, Rev. Mr. Mines visited this city and preached, and organized the Episcopal Society. From the time of the organization of our church there were prayer meetings on Sabbath evenings at the school house, very interesting and largely attended. During the month of August, Mr. C. T. H. Palmer had a day school, which, after suspension, the speaker took up and taught for several weeks, till the rains. A Sabbath school was begun by Prof. Shepherd and carried on afterwards by myself till the rains. Three of those who were in that Sabbath school are yet among us. A certain young lady, still in the city, brought with her over the Plains from Wisconsin a package of Sabbath school books, and these with a set forwarded to myself by Mrs. Dr. Abbe, of Boston, made a very good library: Rev. Mr. Owens arrived in October and took charge of the M. E. Society and got it into shape. A small church building arrived at that time from Baltimore Conference, and that was put up and meetings commenced in it in November. In November Rev. Mr. Wheeler came up from San Francisco and preached, and organized a Baptist church. Rev. Mr. Burnham (Episcopal) came and preached four Sabbaths, was taken sick, lingered through the winter, and died in April, 1850."

From these influences the vicious atmosphere was being almost insensibly transformed, and that public sentiment which was for a few months almost a worshipper of gaming tables was so changed as to lead scores and hundreds who were plunging into ruin into a more careful study of character and a restoration of those more honorable and exalted habits to which they had been educated in youth. These noble messengers of Christian truth had a gigantic task to perform. Under all the disadvantage of a most vitiated and chaotic community they had to proclaim laws which were at total variance with the feelings and desires of the masses. Their messages came indeed "like the voice of one crying from the wilderness," and it was hard to induce people to cordially prepare for the opening of a more substantial and beautiful dispensation. But the power of divine truth was in constant companionship with their efforts, and hence their success. Under this antagonism gambling could not make progress. On the contrary, like wounded error, it is fast "dying amidst its worshippers."

During the spring and summer months an increasing and at last magic progress was being made in the city. All kinds of business were becoming more permanently established, and an aspect of permanency was settling upon everything in and about Sacramento.

At first the principal business was done along Front Street between J and K and in the lower part of J. Shortly after this, while the improvements were extending up J, they were also taking a turn down the river on Front Street and up K to Third. The bank of the river was perfectly crowded with the efforts of landing immigrants and merchandise, and notwithstanding the rapidity with which tents and frame houses were being erected, yet the facilities for storage were totally inadequate, and enormous rates were paid for what could be procured. The bank of the Sacramento soon became lined with vessels devoted to storage, boarding, and lodgings. The principal trading of the city consisted in the purchase and sale of miners' supplies, and one of the most important and lucrative mechanical avocations was that of making rockers. Lumber, as we have before intimated, was scarcely obtainable and, although an enormous price was demanded for it, from fifty cents to one dollar and fifty cents per foot, yet it was bought with an avidity that could scarcely be conceived. Making rockers, building houses, butchering, and baking bread were the great trades of the city at that period. Teaming and packing goods to the mines were employments which absorbed a tremendous amount of energy and enterprise and yielded princely revenues.

In December, '49, fifty dollars per hundred was charged from Sacramento to Mormon Island by teamsters, and up to '52 teaming was one of the most lucrative businesses that could be pursued. In July following, fresh beef sold for fifteen cents per pound, bread fifty cents a loaf the size of a six-penny loaf in New York, butter $2.50 to $3 per pound, cheese $1.5o per pound, corned beef hardly freight, corned pork $20; milk first obtained $1 per quart, dried apples from $1 to $2, saleratus $6 per pound; pickles during the few succeeding months and all kinds of fruit or ascetic [acidic?] vegetables would command almost any price that was demanded.

Carpenters' wages were $16 per day, and laboring men got from $1 to $1.50 per hour. Board during the summer and autumn was for meals alone from $16 to $49 per week; board and lodging, a large increase upon the foregoing rates; washing from $6 to $12 per dozen; physicians' fees from $16 to $32 per visit; medicines, anything that an attenuated conscience could ask. For one ounce of basilicum ointment, $32 was asked and obtained without a murmur.

In the early part of the summer Dr. Cragin, of Washington, D.C., established a hospital at the fort, and the rates of board and attendance at this asylum of Aesculapius were from $16 to $50 per diem. Attorney and court fees were vast improvements upon the charges of medical men as will shortly appear. A glass of liquor cost, at some of the first and elegant resorts, $1; cigars 50 cents a piece; and all indulgences increased in a very rapid ratio until they reached an aspect of such terrible extravagance as to challenge the credulity of men in their sober contemplation of pleasure giving events. Mining implements as follows: rockers, from $50 to $75; shovels, in the fall, $2.75; pickaxes $12; pans $4; small hand gold scales $16 to $32.

About the 4th of July a grand ball was given at the City Hotel, which building was not yet completed. An immense and vigorous effort was made to get up a ball upon a magnificent scale. To do this it was essentially important that every Caucasian descendant of Eve in this section of the state should be present. Accordingly a respectable number of gallant young gentlemen were commissioned to explore the country, with specific instructions to visit every ranch, tent, or wagon bed where there was any indication of feminine divinity, and irrespective of age, cultivation, or grace, to bring one and all to this aristocratic festivity. These orders were admirably attended to, and at the opening of the dance the hungry, rather voracious optics of about two hundred plain looking gentlemen were greeted with the absolute presence of some eighteen ladies, not amazons all, but replete with all the adornments that belong to bold and enterprising pioneers of a new country. Such a sight in California at that time was almost a miraculous exhibition and filled men with such an ebullition of sentiment as to make it impossible to breathe without inhaling the dying cadences of the most devoted and tenderly expressed politeness. Tickets of admission to this ball were $32. The supper was most sumptuously prepared, and champagne circulated so freely that identity became jeopardized and the very illumination of the room converted into a grand magnifying medium for the revels of fancy and delights of illusion.

A gallant young gentleman of the army, who had been specially favored in the dance by one of the ladies, was about to propose her health in a glass of champagne when she anticipated him by presenting her own glass and singing out at the most audible point of voice, "Major, here's to our noble selves." Another gentleman who wished to give a poetic manifestation of his gallantry and who was about to drink with his fair companion in the dance, quoted Moore, where he wishes for a

"Lingering kiss to be left in the glass."

The lady scarcely allowed him to finish the couplet ere she responded, "I shan't do it," and walked off, highly incensed at the politeness extended.

During the month of July a movement was made towards the organization of a city, or rather town, government. The population was rapidly increasing, and a desire for some more familiar or Americanized government began to receive considerable favor. Accordingly, in the latter part of July an election of town councilmen was held at the St. Louis Exchange, in Second Street between I and J. The result was the election of Jno. P. Rodgers, H. E. Robinson, P. B. Cornwall, Wm. Stout, E. F. Gillespie, Thos. F. Chapman, M. T. McClellan, A. M. Winn, and B. Jennings. On the 1st day of August following, the first six gentlemen in the list met at the same place and organized by making Wm. Stout, President, and J. H. Harper, Clerk. The first business coming before this Council was the preparation of a constitution defining the duties of the Council and for the general government of the city. On the 25th of August, A. M. Winn was elected President of the body in place of Stout, who was absent.

On the 20th day of September an election was held at the St. Louis Exchange for the adoption or rejection of a city charter, which had been prepared by the forementioned Council. Prior to the election of these councilmen there was no law or government which was not merely nominal in its character. The only tribunal was an Alcalde's Court in which justice was dispensed with such dispatch and enormous costs that little attention was paid to litigation. Under this regime the people became eminently given to minding their own business and avoiding those legal collisions that are so generally unsatisfying in their results. Consequently when this movement was made to organize a city government, a spirit of opposition began to manifest itself among those who took a little leisure to think of matters that were not directly connected with their business. The opposition principally emanated from the votaries of gaming Hence' when this election came on, the result was much different from what was anticipated by the officials of the city. Upon canvassing the votes it was discovered that the charter had been defeated by a majority of 146 votes.

To the President of the Council, who took a deep and lively interest in the new dispensation of things, this defeat was both un-expected and mortifying. He had exerted himself with a martyr's zeal to imbue the people with a proper conception of their wants and the prospective benefit of a city government, and while reposing upon a platform of conjectured success, he could not seem to understand the capricious and singular phenomenon which this election evolved. In demonstration of this we invite the attention of our readers to the following proclamation, which, emanating from the President of the

Council, makes a most pathetic yet most compromising appeal to the sovereign people as to what they desired the Council to do.

"PROCLAMATION TO THE PEOPLE OF
SACRAMENTO CITY,
BY ORDER OF THE PRESIDENT AND CITY COUNCIL

"On the 1st day of August, 1849, we were elected councilmen of this city, and our powers or duties were not defined. On the 19th of September, following, we presented to you a charter for your consideration which you have seen fit to reject by a majority of 146 votes. Since then we have been unable to determine what the good people of this city desire us to do, and being republicans in principle and having every confidence in the ability of the people to govern themselves, we again request the residents of Sacramento City to meet at the St. Louis Exchange at half-past seven o'clock on Wednesday evening, Oct. l0th, 1849, then and there to declare what they wish the City Council to do. If you wish us to act under the Mexican laws now in force, however inapplicable they may be to our condition, then we must do the best we can; if you have objection to particular features of the charter, then strike out the objectionable features and insert such as you desire. The health and safety of our city demand immediate action on your part, for, in our primitive condition and in the absence of legislative authority, we can in fact be of no service to you without your confidence and consent."

Signed by A. M. Winn, President, and six councilmen."[10]

---

[10] Facsimile of the orginial proclamation reproduced herewith.

PROCLAMATION
TO THE
PEOPLE
OF
SACRAMENTO
CITY,
BY ORDER OF THE
PRESIDENT AND CITY COUNCIL.

On the 1st day of August, 1849, we were elected Councilmen of this City, and our Powers or Duties were not defined. On the 13th day of September, following, we presented to you a Charter for your consideration, which you have seen fit to reject by a majority of 146 votes. Since then we have been unable to determine what the good people of this city desire us to do; and being Republicans in principle, and having every confidence in the ability of the people to govern themselves, we again request the residents of Sacramento City to meet at the ST. LOUIS EXCHANGE, on NEXT WEDNESDAY EVENING, at half past 7 o'clock, then and there to declare what they wish the City Council to do. If you wish us to act under the Mexican Laws now in force, however inapplicable they may be to our condition, then we must do the best we can; if you have objections to particular features of the Charter, then strike out the objectionable features and insert such as you desire. The Health and Safety of our City demand immediate action on your part, for in our primitive condition and in the absence of Legislative authority we can, in fact, be of no service to you without your confidence and consent.

A. M. WINN,
President.

M. T. McCLELLAN,   B JENNINGS,   JOHN P. ROGERS,

T. L. CHAPMAN,   P. B. CORNWALL,   H. E. ROBINSON,

Messrs. E. GILLESPIE - J WM. STOUT Absent

Sacramento City, Oct. 1st, 1849.

3922

The appearance of this official communication added such a climax to the capricious election that all now became interested in what was going on People generally began to inquire about the election of the Council, the presentation and rejection of the charter, and especially about the proclamation which evolved such an earnest appeal to the sympathies of the citizens, for be it known that prior to this singular, this unique condition of municipal government, the apathy of the people to anything outside of their business was so great that few knew whether they were being governed by alcaldes or a Council. The friends of the charter government, being excessively annoyed by the ridiculous position in which things had been placed by the fatal 146 majority, now organized themselves into a party styled the Law and Order Party, and entered most vigorously into the contest in favor of the charter. This was a lucky movement, for the natural negative or antipodes of "law and order" were no law and order, and when with this unfortunate appellative was coupled the universal support of the gambling community, there was little prospect of the no-charter party achieving a second ascendancy.

The election came on pursuant to proclamation, and the result proved the charter party triumphant by a majority of 296 votes. The instrument now adopted was designated the People's Charter, and all the acts of the Council prior to this election, which were not in accordance with the requirement of the charter adopted, were not recognized.

The first charter which was adopted by the Council and rejected by the people was principally repugnant on account of a section in reference to taxation, which authorized the Council to levy and collect taxeswithout the consent of the people. This provision,

Col. Zabriskie informs us, was inserted by the special directions of the Council committee, who were appointed to prepare the charter and who employed Col. Z. to prepare it for them.

The instrument which was finally adopted was a modification of the first one presented and was drawn up by Col. Zabriskie and R. A. Wilson, who were appointed at a general meeting of the citizens for that purpose. The charter reported by these gentlemen, slightly amended by the people, and adopted, was not satisfactory. It had still objectionable powers in respect to taxation, and consequently in the month of December following, another public meeting was called at the Horse Market. At this meeting a committee, consisting of Col. Zabriskie, was appointed to report amendments and restrictions to the existing charter in matters pertaining to taxation, and also to alter so as to require the election of a mayor and recorder. This committee reported to a subsequent meeting, and the charter thus amended was adopted, and Col. Zabriskie and Benj. R. Nickerson were appointed to proceed with said charter to the legislature, then in session, and urge its passage.

The committee here found another charter, which had been prepared by Dr. T. J. White, representative from this district, containing provisions essentially opposed to the charter adopted in meetings referred to, and, by request, both of the instruments provided were referred to the appropriate legislative committee. From this committee a charter was finally reported and became a law, varying but slightly from the one adopted at the Horse Market meeting.

Thus did the city government spring up from the very center of disaffection and apathy. In the first charter election 527 votes were polled against the charter and 381 for it. In the second, 808 were in favor and 513 against.[11]

The city government thus established commenced its feeble efforts to meet the growing and embarrassing wants of the community. Immense responsibilities accumulated upon their shoulders ere they had been given time to acquire the means of action and strength. The rapid concentration of sickness upon the city, the utter and appalling destitution of the incoming adventurers, the terrible reign of cupidity, and the entire absence of all the kind and magic palliatives of home, placed the city government in a most unenviable position. Up to the first of August the city had enjoyed one of those strange immunities from sickness in which it was almost impossible to hear a sound of complaint or to witness the enfeebled and tremulous steps of convalescence. The whole community seemed in a state of health through the spring months and a portion of the summer of this eventful year. Every human being appeared to be reveling in the enjoyment of vigorous energies; every face gleamed with the radiance of unclouded hopes and wild and beautiful dreams of the future. The inconvenience incurred by the burning rays of the sun through the day was neutralized by the cool and renovating atmosphere of night; and the general activity, stimulated into a preternatural buoyancy by the enormous requirements awarded to toil, gave such a tone to appetite, such a power to digestion, and such a

---

[11] The first city charter election occurred on September 20, 1849, when 381 voted for and 527 against adoption. (Sacramento *Placer Times*, Sept. 22, 1849, by a vote of 809 to 527. (Ibid.,Oct. 20, 1849, p. 2, col. 1 A contemporary printed copy of the document is in the Bancroft.)The final charter adopted by the legislature was passed on February 27, 1850, and amended on March 13, 1850. (California Statutes, 1850, p. 70-74, 96-97.)

mellifluous sweetness to sleep, that the whole scene seemed one of enchantment. Thus was it [in] Sacramento ere the rod of affliction was brought to bear upon it in the autumnal months of '49.

At this time Sacramento was a nucleus of attraction to the world. It was the great starting point to the vast and glittering gold fields of California, with the tales of which the whole universe became astounded, and which men of every clime and nation sought to reach without a moment's reflection upon the cost or hazard of such an adventure. The only consideration upon the part of a hundred thousand gold seekers who were preparing for immigration to California was dispatch. Time wasted upon prudential outfits, upon the acquirement of means beyond the passage fee to San Francisco, and peradventure a little spending money to dissipate the impatience of delay was as well wasted in any other way. What were a few dollars that required months to accumulate in the Atlantic States to the gold gleaming ounces that California gave weekly as compensation for the simplest labor?

All men seemed to wish for was the means of setting foot upon California soil, and few were sufficiently provident in their calculations as to provide anything beyond the mere landing at San Francisco. Out of the thousands who landed at the above place in the interval referred to, not one in one hundred arrived in the country with money enough to buy a decent outfit for the mines. Such was the heedlessness with which people ted to this country during the incipient progress of the gold seeking fever. In all parts of the world vessels of every size and condition were put up for the great El Dorado, and as soon as put up were filled to overflow with men who had not the remotest conception of the terrible sufferings they were to encounter.

Along the entire coast of the American continent, in every prominent port of Europe, in nearly every maritime point of Asia, and in nearly all the islands of the world were men struggling with reckless determination for the means of going to California. The earnings of years were instantly appropriated; goods and chattels sold at ruinous sacrifices; homesteads mortgaged for loans obtained upon destructive rates of interest; jewelry, keepsakes, and pension fees pledged for the reimbursement of a beggarly steerage passage for thousands of miles to the town of San Francisco. These are facts with which the world is now familiar, and this being the manner in which people embarked for the Eureka State, it can be easily imagined how those landed who survived the untold and unutterable sufferings endured from port to port. From the first of August, '49, the deluging tides of immigration began to roll into the city of San Francisco their hundreds and thousands daily; not men made robust and hearty by a pleasant and comfortable sea voyage, but poor miserable beings so famished and filthy, so saturated with scorbutic diseases, or so depressed and despondent in spirits as to make them the easy prey of disease and death where they had expected nought but health and fortune.

Thus did mining adventurers pour into San Francisco, nine-tenths of whom, for a few months, immediately took passage to Sacramento. However debilitated they might be, however penniless and destitute, still this, the great focus of mining news, the nearest trading point for miners situated upon a navigable stream, was the only place that men could think of stopping at for recuperative purposes. Hence from Cape Horn, from all the Isthmus routes, from Asiatic seaports, and from the islands of the Pacific, men in the most impoverished health were converging at Sacramento. But these were

61

not the only resources of difficulty to Sacramento in '49. For at the same time that the scurvy-ridden subjects of the ocean began to concentrate amongst us, there was another more terrible train of scorbutic sufferers coming in from the overland roads, so exhausted in strength and so worn out with the calamities of the journey as to be but hardy able to reach this, the Valley City.

From these sources Sacramento became a perfect lazar house of disease, suffering, and death months before anything like an effective city government was organized. It must be recollected that in proportion as these scenes began to accumulate, just in such a proportion did men seem to grow indifferent to the appeals of suffering and to the dictates of benevolence. The more urgent and importunate the cries and beseeching miseries of the sick and destitute, the more obdurate, despotic, and terrible became the reign of cupidity. Everything seemed vocal with the assurance that men came to California to make money, not to devote themselves to a useless waste of time in procuring bread and raiment for the dependent, in watching over and taking care of the sick, or in the burying of the dead The common god (gold!) of that day taught no such feminine virtues, and the king of the country (cupidity) declared it worse than idle in his subjects to pay attention to the ties of consanguinity or stultify their minds with any considerations of affection or appreciation of human sympathies. Fathers paid little attention to sons, and sons abandoned fathers when they required a little troublesome care; brothers were fraternally bound to each other as long as each was equally indepen-dent of all assistance. But when sickness assailed and men became dependents upon men, then it was that the channels of benevolence were found to be dry and the very fountains of human sympathy sealed by the most impenetrable selfishness.

Had this not been the condition, such scenes as were then witnessed could not have been exhibited. If men had not allowed themselves to become the temporary vassals of cupidity, an old grey-headed father, nearly famished by a tedious Cape Horn voyage, and landing upon our levee in the last stage of a disorganizing scurvy, could never have been abandoned by a son and other relatives who were dependent upon him for the means of coming to the country. And yet such an old man was left alone upon the unfrequented banks of the slough to await the corning of the only friends that could give him relief- death and the grave. The grave he was not sure of, but death was certain and soon realized.

In the month of July, '49, these subjects of distress and the appeals of misery became so common that men could not escape them, and if there had been the utmost attention paid to the exercise of charity and protection, it would have been impossible to have met the demands of the destitute, sick, and dying as a commensurate sympathy would have dictated. Such was the difficulty with which facilities for the care of sick people could be procured that even the few who had money could not purchase those comforts which the poorest in the Atlantic States can always enjoy. Dr. Cragin's hospital at the fort was the most comfortable place, but such were the necessary demands for board and nursing that men could not avail themselves of such care. Soon after the establishment of this hospital, Drs. Deal and Martin opened another hospital in one of the bastions of the old fort. This led to a reduction of the cost of hospital board and attendance, but still it was too dear a comfort to be purchased by more than two-tenths of the accumulating invalids of the town. The sick of the city were in consequence thrown upon the exclusive attention of a society which had become so mammon-ridden as to be almost insensible to the voices of want. Not only were the victims of scurvy evolving a general distress, but those who supposed themselves acclimated were beginning to feel the sweeping influences of miasmatic fevers which were peculiarly severe during this first season of affliction to Sacramento.

Under such circumstances, that was true benevolence which attempted to respond to the requirements of humanity. And now let us see where the first grand response to this inexorable appeal came from. The record of so much credit should not perish; the lustre of a humanity that could shine under such circumstances should never depend upon the dim and capricious grasp of recollection to hold it in immortality. It is too effulgent, too beautiful, too winning to be denied a dwelling place in the treasury of a distinct and vivid remembrance.

The first and most effective relief, the first organized efforts "to visit the sick, to relieve the distress, and bury the dead," were made by the fraternity of Odd Fellows! The first lights of effective charity that gleamed upon the despairing visions of hundreds of the sick and dying ascended from the altar fires of this glorious brotherhood which the presiding genius of the institution had enkindled. Although denied the privilege of a complete organization, they yet came together, bound themselves by an informal association, and like a band of pure Samaritans, devoted themselves with untiring zeal to the wants and necessities of suffering humanity. Gen. A. M. Winn was elected President of the association, than whom no man could have been more active in his charity, a Mr. McLaren, Secretary, and Capt. Gallup,

Treasurer. And every member of this body became one of a visiting committee whose duty it was to keep the society constantly advised of every dependent subject of distress coming to their knowledge.

From this association, the history of which would thrill the heart of every lover of humanity, an immense and immeasurable amount of relief was dispensed. But this was not sufficient to dissipate the increasing calamity. Men still sickened and died without assistance; men were still buried in the filth of unattended sickness and frequently without the benefit of being sewed up in a blanket for interment. Rough pine coffins ranged from $60 to $150, and it was not to be expected that in the midst of such distress and poverty, coffins could be always procured. The association of Odd Fellowship spent thousands of dollars for coffins alone; and when Gen. Winn became the executive officer of the city government, no man was refused a coffin burial.

Drs. Taylor and Hazzard opened a canvas hospital in K Street between Second and Third, but still the prices of board did not fall below $16 per diem, and the supply of nurses and blankets was so limited, and the effect of a hot sun upon the canvas roof so severe, that it was little better than the open air beneath the protecting foliage of trees and shrubbery.

We will now return to the doings of the City Council and give as much of the record of their proceedings as our space and haste will admit.

On the 16th of October, Dr. T. J. White, who with his interesting family had arrived in the city a few weeks before, was elected a member of the Council in place of Stout, who had left the town.

On the 17th of October, Col. J. B. Starr petitioned the Council in behalf of an ordinance for the regulation of auctioneering licenses. November 5th, Jacob R. Snyder was admitted to the Council to fill a vacancy occasioned by M. T. McClellan's absence, and Wm. Glaskins was elected Clerk in place of Flarper, resigned. Drs. White and Chapman and Mr. Rogers were appointed a committee to aid and assist the sick at the expense of the Council. On the 12th of November an ordinance defining the duties of officers and creating new offices was adopted, and the following persons appointed to positions: R. J. Watson, Flarbor Master; Murray Morrison, City Attorney; N. C. Cunningham, Marshal; Charles A. Miller, Deputy Marshal; John Lacroze, Assessor; B. Brown, Tax Collector; S. C. Hastings, City Treasurer; E. Crosby, Coroner; C. W. Coote, Engineer.

November 22d, E. J. C. Kewen and Mr. Smith were appointed members of the Council in place of Messrs. Jennings and Robinson.

We have before intimated that the attorneys' fees were much higher than were charged by medical gentlemen. This fact is deducible from the following bill of a legal gentleman, presented to the Council on the 20th of November:

To drawing ordinance, relating to the occupation
        of public streets, alleys, etc. ....$ 100
To drawing up city charter.. 1,000
To drawing ordinance, relating to
        public officers and their duties......................   200
To three hearings, and two arguments
        in the case of *City of Sacramento vs. Jinness*............   *500*
To preparation of ordinance for streets,
        by order of committee, but not called for..........   200
To advice at different times and for various subjects
        by committee of City Council......................   500

                             Total $2,500

This bill, which we believe was not extraordinarily high, was, for cause not appearing, reduced by the Council to $680.

November 24th, Dr. Myles was elected to the Council, in place of the vacancy made by the resignation of P. B. Cornwall.

On the 28th of November the following rates of license were adopted by the Council, to wit:

Tax on wholesale and retail dealers, in merchandise per month............	$ 50
Tax on retail dealers in merchandise.........................	25
Tax on hotel or eating houses................................	50
Tax on faro or gaming tables, each.........................	30
Tax on billiard tables (one in city)	10
Tax on auctioneers with merchants' license.................	25
Tax on auctioneers without merchants' license..............	50
Tax on exchange brokers, &c.	50
Tax on theater..	20
Tax on concerts or public entertainment.....................	5
Tax on public drays or carts.................................	5
Tax on hawkers or peddlers of goods, &c..................	20
Tax on meat markets..	50

On the 23d of September the first rain of the season took place. Through the ensuing month of October the rains became much more severe, cold, and accompanied with heavy winds. No adequate preparation had been made to shield the citizens from this new element of disturbance, and every exertion was at once made to provide warm and comfortable shelter. The early setting in of the rainy season aggravated to an indescribable degree the miseries of the sick and destitute. Fevers were now making their appearance, and in consequence of the general debility and previous prostrations induced, they assumed a low and perilous type; yet such was the lack of shelter that many cases of severe typhus fever were lying in such exposed situations that their bed clothing would be saturated with the piercing rains prevailing generally during the nights of that year. And still they did sometimes recover. Everybody who could avail himself of the necessary means began to erect more substantial and drier buildings; and notwithstanding the enormous prices asked for lumber, yet stores and hotels were run up as if by magic. The rents at this time [were] becoming so exorbitant as to put it beyond the power of men to rent without an immense capital or a large business with the heaviest conceivable profits.

After the rains set in and after having witnessed the terrible situation of the sick, Drs. Morse and Stillman succeeded in getting the most commodious hospital erected in California at that time, by Barton Lee. Plans for a hospital were constructed by these parties, the probable income and expenditure estimated, and the urgent necessity of such a resort for invalids presented to various men then engaged in building, but to no purpose. The last application was made to Barton Lee. He distrusted the enterprise as a speculation but had his sympathies so excited by a representation of the miseries around him that he consented to put up the building demanded at once. Never did Barton Lee perform a more noble act. On the corner of K and Third streets he had constructed in an inconceivably short time a story-and-a-half building, 40 x 50 feet. This was immediately opened by the forementioned physicians, and the price of hospital board and attendance reduced to $10 per day. The rent of the building was fixed at $1,500 per month, which for the capital invested was probably the lowest rent in the city. The proprietors of this hospital made an effort to get those sick to take care of for which the city became responsible, at the same rate, but the Council preferred to remove their patients to the fort and pay $16 per day for vastly inferior accommodations.

This led to considerable agitation upon the subject of building a hospital, and the Council determined to erect a building for that purpose upon the public square between I and J and 9th and 10th streets, 20 x 60 feet, two stories high. The estimated cost of the building was $14,000. The records of the Council show that warrants to the amount of $7,000 were drawn and placed in the hands of the chairman of the committee for the purchase of lumber, etc., in the prosecution of this enterprise, but unfortunately the building had not been sufficiently completed to withstand the severe storms that were now prevailing, in one of which it was prostrated to the ground and the timber so injured as to make it almost useless for future building purposes.

Soon afterwards the Council procured the use of Dr. White's unique gothic cottage on L Street, which consisted of a small frame front building and a canvas extension in the rear. Into this place a large number of sick were crowded, some of whom were near being drowned in the January flood.

About the first of December, Capt. Jno. A. Sutter donated ten acres of ground to the city for a graveyard—the present cemetery of Sacramento. [12]

On the 7th day of December, H. A. Schoolcraft petitioned the Council to remove a house built by Charles Robinson upon property

---

[12] This is still the Sacramento City Cemetery, situated at the end of 10th Street and south of Broadway.

which he represented. Prior to the reception of this petition, a few men in the city, calling themselves squatters, had been agitating the question of Capt. Sutter's title to the land upon which the city had been located. This Charles Robinson was among the first to practically demonstrate his non-belief in Sutter's title by settling upon and claiming the lot in question. The lot was situated on the levee near I Street and regarded as public ground. The city authorized the removal, and the feeling excited in the community against the squatters made the removal of the building a scene too much of gratification and rebuke to be forgotten by the contestants.

The next day a suit was entered against the city for the removal of this private property, which resulted in favor of the city. This brings us to a subject that is so much a part of our city's history that it cannot be passed over without comment, and which to be understood should be truthfully stated.

In the early part of the fall of '49, certainly not later than the first of October, men began to say that Sutter's title to the property on which the city was located was not good, that the property was public land and consequently subject to all the privileges of preemption. At first this idea was promulged by a few illiterate and uninfluential men who were treated by the speculators in town lots and the general owners of property with the most unmeasured contempt. This treatment, while it suppressed for a short time the boldness of the squatters, did not by any means extinguish the spirit. At that time the squatters began to intimate that they would receive such a reinforcement when the immigration arrived as to secure them in their possession of property upon which they settled.

This was to a certain degree the result of the arrival of immigrants who crossed the Plains. Worn out by a long journey, without money or home, less scrupulous and more selfish as people inevitably become after a long succession of hardships, they did not listen with indifference to the assurance that by the mere locating [of] their tent upon a city lot it became thereby their property. Thus in a very few weeks the timid and esteemed insignificant squatterism became what it now is, a distinct party organization. Lots were staked off in many parts of the city, and the squatter's title boldly presented as a superior claim to one which was based upon a purchased title through the conveyance and sub-conveyances of Capt. John A. Sutter. But before we proceed to narrate any of the prominent events occurring from this land title antagonism, we would like the question of city squatterism and city Sutterism to be presented in its naked relations to facts. In this way every man will be qualified for drawing his own conclusions and morally responsible for the equity and justice of his opinions. And as it is a question identified with riot and blood-shed in the history of our city, a question yet unsettled and heavily influencing the general elections of the state, it cannot be too well understood. We mean of course in its absolute moral relations.

Capt. John A. Sutter claimed the land which is now embraced within the limits of this city through grants from the Mexican gov-ernment and through the guarantees of the treaty of the United States with Mexico. His claim is sustained by an adjacent settlement, by immense and, at the time, most useful improvements, and the occasional occupation of the present site of the city. Also by a purchased survey by a person whom he supposed to be a competent engineer, and an accompanying map, both of which located him upon the place he claimed. Upon this claim, so sustained, he conveyed the property to his son, John A. Sutter, Jr., from whom it has been purchased and sold and passed through the hands of thousands of individuals.

Against this claim the squatters urged that the natural boundaries of the land claimed were not in keeping with the imaginary lines or the boundaries of latitude and longitude which were given by the engineer; that Capt. Sutter had not complied with the requisitions of his grants; and especially that the site of the city could not be embraced within the land granted, as by the stipulations of the grant the land embraced was not to be subjected to annual inundations; and that by the improvement of Hock Farm and New Helvetia he had overstepped the boundaries of his possessions per grants either to the north or south ; and as the engineer had given the southern boundary by latitudinal lines, and as those lines, when correctly taken, placed his southern limit considerably above this point; therefore this, the site of Sacramento, was public land and subject to pre-emption possession by occupation and improvement. The first civil suit against the squatters was instituted in November, 1849, by *Jno. A. Sutter et al. vs. Geo. Chapman.* A writ of restitution was issued by Judge Thomas and served by Presley Dunlap.

These were the leading issues that were first developed in the fall of '49 between the squatters and anti-squatter parties. The removals alluded to from the public grounds gave great umbrage to the squatters and were not forgotten by them, although the incoming rainy season and the terrible flood gave a temporary quietus to the subject.

72

During the month of October, '49, the first theater in Sacramento was erected on Front Street between I and J, of canvas material, and named Eagle Theater. It was built by Mr. Hubbard and opened under the management, we believe, of Mr. Atwater. The admission to this place of amusement was $5 and, as a place of entertainment, was not only well supported but, we believe, contributed to improve the condition of society that prevailed at the time. Following this humble effort to develop dramatic exhibitions was a much more extensive one in the spring succeeding, by Messrs. McDowell, Fowler, and Warbass. They erected the Tehama frame theater which was located on Second Street between I and J and opened under the management of Mr. Wingard, the then husband of Mrs. James Stark.

The success of this begot a sort of theater fever which led to the erection of the Pacific Theater by Messrs. Queen and Petit on M Street near Front. This place was opened by Charles R. Thorne.

One of the first enterprises begun after the town was really developed as a substantial place was steamboating. As early as July, 1849, Capt. John Van Pelt, who became a sort of Pacific Vanderbilt, had built the *Sacramento* steamboat at Washington, or rather on the opposite bank of the river."[13] With this flat bottomed scow, representative of Fulton's extensive progeny, he made several trips to San Francisco and back, but his principal beat was between Sacramento and New York of the Pacific. She rated at about 40 tons burthen.

---

[13] Washington, now Broderick, was located on the western bank of the Sacramento River, opposite Sacramento. The town was not laid out until February, 1850.

In the month of October, '849, this same heroic engineer and pioneer in Sacramento steamboating made his entrance into our city as commander of the magnificent old *Senator* upon her first trip up the river. All the nymphs of the ocean making their appearance in our midst would not have excited more rejoicing and enthusiasm than did this noble floating palace. It sat upon the Sacramento so much like the old *Knickerbocker* upon the Hudson; it infused such a vitality into our mercantile relations with San Francisco; it demonstrated so unequivocally the entire navigability of the beautiful river upon which our city's destiny depended; it gave assurance of so much comfortable journeying and imparted such a feeling of home to everybody and everything that came near it, that there was substantial reason for all the enthusiasm and jollification excited by its presence. She commenced making regular trips, up one day and down the next, and did as much business as she was capable of at $30 passage money and $35 per ton for freight. Her officers were John Van Pelt, captain; Chas. Van Pelt, mate; Andrew Hallet, clerk; Wm. E. Bushnell, pilot ; Mr. Griffith, engineer. This splendid and most successful boat was brought out by the instrumentality and enterprise chiefly of Lieut. Maynard of the U. S. Navy.

We believe that the *M'Kim*, commanded by Capt. Brenham, anticipated the *Senator* several weeks, but a glance at the make of the vessel and her acknowledged sluggishness did not secure for her a reception such as was accorded to the comparatively gorgeous *Senator.* She, however, became a splendid source of revenue in the river trade, especially in the carrying of freight. Following these in rapid succession came the *Hartford*, commanded by Capt. Averill, in December, '49; the *Gold Hunter, El Dorado,,New World,,* and in the winter of 1850, the *New*

Orleans, under the command of Capt. Wakeman, which was soon withdrawn and put on the Panama route. The *Confidence*, *Antelope*, and *Wilson G. Hunt* were not long in following in the wake of the forementioned steamers, and thus in an incredibly short time the Sacramento River was converted into an arm of commerce and trade that will at some future period vie with the far famed channel of commercial intercourse between New York and Albany.

On the 12th of December the Council became so intensely affected with that species of charity which "begins at home" that they adopted an ordinance paying each member $100 per month for his services. This act of the Council created quite a feeling among the constituency and rendered the body for a time not a little unpopular and uninfluential. The Council, however, succeeded very soon to render a partial atonement for their self-paying propensity by manifesting an active interest in the relief of immigrants. The season was becoming so dreadfully inclement that relief was indispensable. The Odd Fellows were now joined in their herculean efforts to take care of the destitute and sick by another association of the most glorious and noble character, the Free Masons. But these combined exertions could not meet the full wants of a community so terribly scourged as Sacramento. Nor could the Council in itself complete the task of relief which these magnificent, these sacred and humane orders had commenced. These orders contributed money and appropriated exertions as freely as if their lives had been devoted to the exclusive function of human kindness. And it is not strange that in 1853 these two associations of benevolence should occupy so exalted a position as they enjoy. Their fair names are inscribed in indelible and living characters upon those pages of history which California must preserve.

They could not do all that was to be done, nor could the associated help of the Council respond to the increasing wants of the invalid exiles.

The Council at this time called a public meeting, and the President of the Council made a most urgent appeal to the people in mass to come forward and assist in the general effort at relief. The President was dispatched to Monterey for the purpose of laying our necessities before Gen. Riley and procuring from him, if possible, some of the public funds then in his possession. This mission was un-availing. Gen. Riley, the Military Governor of the territory, did not consider himself in possession of the right to make such an appropriation of the national funds.

Sacramento was therefore thrown back again upon her own limited resources to meet contingencies worthy of a nation's benevolence. To say that she did not do all that might have been done to assuage the widespread misery that environed her would be no reproach. All that she could do was most cordially, most readily performed. Her treasury was empty, her credit in that unsettled period at a necessarily low ebb, and the hand that is palsied from poverty cannot be very bounteous nor steady in its administration of substantial charity. If, as a corporation, she "had no soul," she did, as a corporation, have eyes that wept over those calamities that were bowing down some of the noblest men that ever wandered from a hospitable home.

By her co-operation with individual efforts and the vigorous benevolence of the aforesaid fraternities, she succeeded in furnishing a tolerable shelter, food, and medical attendance for the sick, and especially did she put an end to those terrible burials which were made at an earlier date, without coffins, and in some cases without even a blanket protection from the disorganizing influences of an most saturated earth.

But the trying difficulties which Sacramento was now realizing ere nothing to what she was soon thrown into by the relentless flood that took place on the 8th day of January following. For this dreadful enemy, coming like a thief in the night, she had made no provision. The reckless spirit of speculation had declared an inundation as out of the question, if not physically impossible. The very air was tremulous with oft repeated assurances that the town plot had remained free from floods during the sojourn of the oldest Californians, and the headlong and unreflecting career of the people rowed them sufficiently credulous to believe the really transparent story.

Thus, persons who would have otherwise raised their buildings so as to have given them some security, or fastened their merchandise in order to prevent its being swept from their reach, were induced to build upon the ground, whatever the topography of the lot on which improvements were erected. And as will always be the case when the relative height of lots is estimated by the eye, hundreds of persons who supposed themselves to be upon elevated grounds found that they were the first to be submerged by the inrushing waters of 1850. The rains through the latter part of December and first of January were so heavy that men began to entertain an apprehension of approaching difficulty. The Sacramento River and the American Fork were rising rapidly, and the back country seemed to be fast filing up and cutting off communication from the high lands.

But still every one was inclined to believe the ridiculous and false assurances of safety, which could scarcely be extinguished when the city was absolutely under water. And hence, when the deluging waters began to rush in and overwhelm the city, there was no adequate means of escape for life or property; and consequently many were drowned, some in their beds, some in their feeble efforts at escape; and many died in consequence of the terrible exposures to which they were necessarily subjected. The few boats which belonged to the shipping moored by the levee were brought into immediate requisition in gathering up the women, children, and invalids that were scattered over the city in tents and canvas houses. Some of the women who were living in tents situated in remote low places were found standing upon beds and boxes in water a foot and a half deep and which was still rising with perilous rapidity. Sick men, totally helpless, were found floating about upon cots that seemed miraculously buoyant, and in the enfeebled tones of dissolution crying for help.

The hospital then used by the authorities was the frame and canvas house first occupied by Dr. White. It was unfortunately situated upon very low ground, and in the temporary absence of the attending physician was entirely abandoned by those who could have been of service to the poor invalids during the aggressions of the water. By mere accident, a boat in which Capt. J. Sherwood was manager passed the hospital and discovered the situation of the floating sick by their dreadful cries for help. The boat was immediately appropriated to the office of removing them to a vacant house of Mr. Samuel Brannan, where they were at least safe from drowning.

During the time that these invalids were remaining in the store of Mr. Brannan, occupied by Petit as a lumber yard, many of them died, and Messrs. Boyd and Davis made coffins for them. They used to send a Dutchman and another individual out with the corpses to bury them, in one of their boats. The Dutchman was very suspicious of everybody so far as his money was concerned and consequently carried it about his person, in gold dust. This he had accumulated to the amount of two thousand dollars when, unfortunately, he made a mistake upon one of his burying commissions and placed the coffin with the corpse across their smallest boat. The two got in and succeeded in getting some distance into deep water when the boat commenced careening and finally sank. The Dutchman, who was a powerful swimmer, cried to his companion, who was holding on to the coffin, "holt on, swim ashore and get a boat." He had not swum but a short distance when the weight of the gold dust drew him under water. By a tremendous struggle he came up again and struck out anew, but only to repeat he sinking and rising several times and finally to sink forever into a death which he preferred to detaching and losing the gold dust upon his person. The other was saved by the buoyancy of the coffin, which had been made very tight.

We believe there were between twelve and twenty removed to his place on the levee, only two of which number revived from the unutterable sufferings they had endured. After the death of a majority of them, the balance was removed by order of Capt. Sherwood and consent of the authorities to the hospital on the corner of K and Third streets. One of these thus removed was an old man who had become a mere skeleton from a chronic diarrhoea. With assistance his thread-bare coat and pants were removed and by request hung up by his cot. In a few hours afterwards one of the physicians going up to see him discovered that his coat and pants had changed their color from a black to a light and decidedly living grey, and upon a little closer inspection the grey was found to depend upon a perfect coating of those execrable animals technically called pediculæ and of that abominable species that prefer a habitation upon the bodies of neglected or filthy individuals. But his situation was less revolting than a number of the many victims to disease and despicable neglect which were crowded into the second story of this hospital on the night of the flood. From a miserable canvas building on K. Street between Second and Third called a hospital, opened by Drs. Hazzard and Taylor and subsequently kept by Hazzard, the most dreadful representatives of a worse than heartless neglect were rescued from the invading waters and thrust into the above frame hospital on the opposite corner. Three were brought at one boat load, rolled up in the blankets in which they had been lying no one could tell how long, but certainly in a condition too horrible to be seen and too awful to meet a faithful description. One of them whose blanket enveloped the entire body and head seemed to be rapidly dying, and consequently he was the first to get the attention of the physicians and nurses. An attempt was made to unroll the blanket, but it was found to be so adherent to many parts of the body as to make it difficult of removal—so difficult that the effort was delayed, after the face was relieved, for the deplorable victim to revive if possible, or if not that death might free him from a sense of his situation. Fortunately for him, death was the speedy alternative. His troubles were ended. A finely developed form, a face on which lingered the indices of cultivated intellect, a heart that once beat with manly pride, were enwrapped in a death so dreadful as to beggar description and so appalling as to excite an almost eternal impression of nausea and disgust in the minds of those who beheld it. The blanket was with difficulty detached and when drawn off presented a shirtless body already partially devoured by an immense bed of maggots

80

occupying nearly as much space as the emaciated carcass itself. And when one adds to this loathsome mass, these crawling elements of disgust, the accumulated excretions which were alike confined by the agglutinated folds of the blanket, a head of hair almost clogged up with vermin, then can a just conception be formed of what was suffered during the sickness of the fall and winter of '49. This, which was probably the worst case of the interval referred to, was too nearly approached by many of the victims of an impoverished exilement. Where the best efforts were made to promote cleanliness, with men who had fortunes at their command, it was almost impossible to avoid an exhibition of scenes that would appal the heart of any man who had been reared amid the comforts and cleanliness of eastern homes. Many might suppose that under such circumstances, when disease was rioting in the community, when seven-tenths of the population were valetudinarians, that physicians were piling up fortunes through professional assessments. But nothing could be further from the truth. Their professional knowledge became fountains of charity, entailing upon them not only the motives and means of doing good but in many instances associated appeals that consumed alike their previous savings and even their wardrobes in the vain effort to assuage the misery and distress which they could not fly from. We say fly from, for it was the instinctive habit of those whose professions or official positions did not require them to visit the sick, to avoid all knowledge of the sufferings around them.

Hence, at 10 o'clock on the evening of the flood, when the backwaters of the sloughs and the waters that came pouring in from the banks of the Sacramento were rushing into the city, tearing up sidewalks and dislodging merchandise, sweeping away tents and upsetting houses; at this very time and throughout the inundation the city seemed almost mad with boisterous frolic, with the most irresistible disposition to revel in all the joking, laughing, talking, drinking, swearing, dancing, and shouting that were ever patronized by the wine drinking son of Jupiter and Semele.

All the shipping and two story houses became crowded with the unwebbed bipeds of hilarity and merriment. When hundreds of thousands of dollars in merchandise were being wrested from the grasp of the merchants and traders of our city by the sweeping currents that were running through the streets in some places with irresistible force, no man could have found among the losers of property a single dejected face or despondent spirit. There were no gloomy consultations, no longing looks cast upon the wakes of absconding produce, no animosities excited. Brannan, Cornwall, Lee, Hensley, Reading, Fowler, and a score of others whose enterprise had fixed the local destiny of the town, and who were so artlessly skeptical as to the possibility of inundation, were the peculiar spirits of congeniality and the decided favorites of the aquatic yet unamphibious community. A man who would purposely roll into the water that he might share the general laugh that was entailed upon one who had accidentally fallen in would not wet the sole of his foot or disturb a joke to save a barrel of his pork that was being carried off by the current.

In the early part of this great flood small boats would bring almost any price on sale or hire. A common sized whale boat would bring $30 per hour and sell readily for $1,000; but in an incredibly short time every particle of lumber that would answer for boat or raft making was thus appropriated; and in a few days the people were en abled to emigrate to the adjacent hills, where settlements were made similarly to the Hoboken of 1853. [14]

At the time that this sudden inundation was effecting its destruction to life and property, the City Council were most commendably at work making vigorous and untiring efforts to relieve the distressed and unprotected. The Council were seconded in their exertions by all who had means and especially by those who had places of refuge to offer. Almost every second story was freely appropriated to the occupancy of the needy.

It would be impossible to estimate the amount of property destroyed by this terrible visitation. The flood occurred at a time when there were not, less probably than three hundred persons engaged pretty extensively in business; and of these there were not more than five or six who had second stories for storing goods and perhaps an equal number not entirely flooded on the first story. The balance were obliged to see their effects floated off to destruction or nearly ruined by the water that inundated them in the stores.

Among the most prominent business men in the city at that time were Hensley & Reading; Brannan & Sherwood; Starr, Bensley & Co.; Priest, Lee & Co.; Wesley Merritt; Fowler & Fry; McNulty & Brother; J. B. Starr & Co.; Earl, McIntosh & Co.; Moran & Clark; E. D. & W. D. Kennedy; Cavert & Co.; John Hatch; Freeman & Co.'s Express; Simmons, Hutchinson & Co.;—Stephens; J. L. L. F. Warren; H. E. Robinson & Co.; R. Gelsten; Orlando McKnight; Powers &

---

[14] Norristown, later Hoboken, was laid off in February, 1850, a few miles above Sacramento on the American River. (Sacramento *Placer Times*, Feb. 23, 1850, p. 3, col. 2) During the flood of Jan., 1853, while Sacramento was cut off from the mines, local merchants established temporary branch stores there, but to no evidence now remains.

Perkins; Haines, Webster & Co.; Boyd & Davis; A. P. Petit; Geo. H. Johnson; L. P. & S. S. Crane; D. O. Mills & Co.;— Barlow; Meconnekin & Co.; John Van Houghton; Brown, Henry & Co.; James Lea; William M. Carpenter; Thompson & Taylor; Jacob Binninger, Cochran; —Peifer; Samuel Gregg; S. C. Bruce; Montgomery & Co.; Capt. Gallup; A. M. Winn; B. F. Hastings; A. C. Latson; Ames & McKenzie; Jesse Haycock; Dearbower; Caswell, Ingalls & Co.; Hanna, Jennings. & Co.; Henley & Birdsall; Capt. Northam; Demas Strong; Wilcoxson & Co.; Geise & Son; Nevett & Co.; J. J. Burge; Robert Burge; Hardenbergh & Co.; Morrill & Harnlin;—Youmans; C. C. Sackett; Kibbe, Almy & Co.;; Coates & Rivett; Spalding & Martin ;— Cheeks ;—Pinckard ;—Hermance ;— Prince; H. Arents & Co.; Scranton & Smith; T. S. Mitchell & Co.; Reynolds & Co.; R. Chenery.

Nearly all of these men were severe losers by this unexpected calamity. But it did not bow them into despondency. That iron energy of character with which they were endowed gave them the power of reaction as soon as the force of the storm had subsided. Men did not then estimate their strength by any of the advantages of the past. The present as a fulcrum and the future as a lever constituted die power with which they were most familiar. With these elements of strength, immense results could be accumulated in a short and almost magic period of time.

In a few days after the flood had deluged the city the sky became again clear and beautiful, day and night. And this condition of weather continued with trivial interruptions until the succeeding heavy rains of the March following Under the influence of this agreeable change the waters began rapidly to abate, so that in a few days some of the stores and hotels on Front and J streets were enabled to enter into a brisk and profitable business again; and during the month of February a communication with the mines was reopened, and the city presented an appearance so cheerful and busy as to induce a general forgetfulness of past losses. But although the losses were seemingly forgotten, yet the inundation had excited a great deal of interest in the subject of future defense against floods. Such, however, was the infatuated determination to believe the cool reiterations of the speculators in respect to the liability of the city to be inundated, that a few weeks only were required to induce a confidence of future security almost as great as that which had been manifested prior to the flood. A few people allowed themselves to cherish a little skepticism upon the subject, and, engaging in building soon after, they elevated their foundations above high water mark; but their position being not only an eccentric one but exceedingly inconvenient, some of them were really induced to lower their buildings just in time to be a second time submerged by the spring inundation.

A few men would be occasionally expressing a fear that the melting snows of spring together with the rains would cause another overflow and many were induced to talk upon the subject of defense by a levee. But with northern men and men upon the Atlantic board generally, a levee was a species of fortification in respect to which they knew about as much as New Englanders know concerning the vegetable characteristics of gumbo But nothing could exceed the unpopularity of this project both with northern and southwestern men.

It seemed to be a general impression that an inundation would take place about as quickly by a process of percolation or by the capillary action of water upon the soil as by being poured into the city over the banks of the river. This idea was therefore too unpopular to be often urged. But in the month of March following, heavy rains occurred which, with the increased action of the sun upon the snow summits, caused another flood. The rivers rose with great rapidity, the sloughs filled up to the overflowing, and the city must have been nearly as severely flooded as in January but for the masterly and herculean efforts of Hardin Bigelow. This man had declared from the first in favor of the practicability of defending the city by a levee. Having thus committed himself to the proposition, he was determined to demonstrate his theory in this second flood. With a moiety of means and a handful of men he commenced damming up the intruding waters at every low point and finally extended his temporary levee almost to its present limits. Night and day he was in his saddle, going from one point to another and stimulating his men to an almost superhuman action. For a few days this man met tide and torrent, mud and darkness, and croaking discouragements that few men in the world could have endured, and to the utter astonishment of all he saved the town from a severe inundation. J, Front, Second, I, and a portion of K streets he kept open for the uninterrupted transaction of business. As a natural consequence everybody praised him, and on the first Monday of April succeeding, at an election held pursuant to the new legislative charter adopted February 27th, 1850, he was elected with a most cordial vote as the chief magistrate of this city.

In addition to his election at the time referred to: B. F. Washington, Recorder; J. Neely Johnson, City Attorney; N. C. Cunningham, Marshal; Barton Lee, Treasurer; J. W. Woodland, Assessor. And Messrs. J. R. Hardenbergh, V. Spalding, D. Strong, C. H. Miller, Thos. McDowell, C. A. Tweed, A. P. Petit, and Drs. Moore and Mackenzie, councilmen. On the ensuing May 21st, James Queen was elected to fill a vacancy occasioned by the resignation of C. H. Miller.

The Council elected the following officers, to-wit: J. B. Mitchel, Clerk; George W. Hammersly, Harbor Master, with one deputy; Dr. V. Spalding, City Physician; E. B. Pratt, Collector; and J Stanley, Measurer of Lumber.

In a few weeks after the abatement of the waters of the second inundation, everything seemed almost transformed into business and money making. The new Council were busily engaged with the subject of a levee, surveys were made, and every avenue of wealth was opened, and a man had nothing to do but take his stand in some useful employment and realize the income of a prince. Tents, canvas houses, and diminutive frames gave place to large and most commodious stores and houses built of good mated and ornamented and beautified by architectural embellishments. Business began to assume something like system; the most rapid revolutions were constantly taking place in trade; teaming became an extensive source of emolument; stage lines were constructed and permeated every prominent valley leading to mining regions; parties and dinners, bull fights and horse races, theaters, Sabbath schools, and sewing circles all began an emulation for patronage, but we cannot say with an equality of success. The more moral and religious the vying interest, the more difficult its progress. At that time there was a wonderful scarcity of swine in this section of California, and the devil, having no refuge, abided by the sons of Jonathan. Hence the utter recklessness of manners, the deterioration of tastes, and the disgusting abandonment of Americanism for the semi-civilized habits of the great Greaser

87

family and the almost imitation of Digger Indians. To our mind nothing could have been more debasing to real Americanism than the sickening exchange of a respectable cloak or overcoat for a miserable, striped-looking, torn blanket called a serape— a disfiguring of the face with an overgrowth of half washed hair, pantaloons composed of half white muslin and half velvet childishly ornamented with hundreds of bell-buttons, red sash, and unsightly appendages to the heels called spurs made of huge spikes slightly polished fixed in a gingling cylinder.

But whatever may have been the moral derelictions of Californians at this period, one thing is most certain, that the spring and first summer months of '50 were marked by such evolutions of trade and exchange, such purchases and sales as have seldom been seen by any member of the human family. This season of business developed some of the more substantial mercantile houses and manufacturing firms and, we may say, some of the strongest banking houses of the country. The city improved so rapidly as to astound strangers and beget a lively interest in the prospective importance of the town. The seasons in which this state of business was developed were extraordinarily exempt from disease. The almost innumerable physcans of the previous period of maladies were compelled to abandon pills and powders and take to the less congenial employment of mining. Their calling seemed for the time to be almost gone. But this career of an indescribable and wonderful progress was destined too soon to be interrupted. The very air became freighted with the moral elements of strife and discord that revelled in revulsion of confidence, prosperity, and security. But before we enter into a con- sideration of those incidents which indicated the approaching storms, we will glance at some of the prominent acts of the Council and other matters of interest to the general record.

During the months of April, May, and June the Council seemed to have had but little to attend to. Among the first prominent resolutions of this board of city fathers we find the following chivalric tribute of kindness to a terpsichorean troupe:

"July 5th, 1850. On motion of Alderman Tweed, it was resolved by the City Council that the thanks of the Council be tendered to a ballet troupe now in this city for the pleasant entertainment Wednesday evening last to which this body was invited. And resolved that the clerk transmit a copy of this resolution to the manager of the ballet troupe."

July 7th, resolutions of a most eulogistic character were adopted by the board in reference to the triumph of Hardin Bigelow over the second high waters, in March.

On the 16th of July the Council turned their attention to the organization of a fire department and made contributions towards le purchase of an engine.

July 27th, the attention of the city was called to the condition of immigrants by the Plains. Public meetings were held very frequently and large subscriptions made for the relief of the sick and destitute who commenced arriving by this route. Among the most prolific sources of revenue at this time was the Rancho of Col. Joseph Grant upon the levee. He gave nightly soirees, and by his unique system of organizing his meetings and monopolizing all the offices to himself, as well as by his witty harangues, he performed a function of benevolence for which he has never been adequately appreciated."[15]

About this period of intensely warm weather a cargo of ice arrived, Never did a congenial visitant receive a more melting and *spirited* welcome. A thousand thirsting stomachs excited the recollection of bygone refreshments and imbued as many minds with an irresistible fancy for cocktails, cobblers, and juleps. The Council, which vas composed of men to whom smiles were peculiarly agreeable, voted the vessel a free berth during her delivery.

The assessor's report on the value of property, real estate and personal, gave an aggregate of $7,968,985. This is a most important report as it conveys a full and specific explanation of the terrible pecuniary revulsion to which we were tending. The real estate alone of the city was assessed at $5,586,000, probably full $5,000,000 over the true intrinsic value of the property at that time; and yet such was the inflated and ruinous estimates of the day, such the unbounded confidence in the prevailing standards of calculation, that men skilled in the science of money lending regarded property at this enormous valuation as a sufficient guaranty of payment.

Hence, following the financial reaction of the fall of '50s, some of the shrewdest men in the community found themselves

---

[15] Eccentric Col. Joseph Grant, auctioneer, real estate agent, newsdealer, had an establishment near the embarcadero. He could "rattle off anything, town lots, literature and matches in a most happy manner for cash." Agent for lots n the new town of Nicolaus—formerly Nicolaus Ranch—California correspondent and agent for the *True Delta* of New Orleans, early day public relations specialist, he was more than an ordinary eccentric. His name was repeatedly linked with civic projects requiring the raising of funds. Early in 1850 he was the unsuccessful candidate for mayor on the "Rancho Ticket," afterwards, characteristically declaring he would stump the state for the governorship.

severely embarrassed by immense losses accruing from loans on real estate. Mortgages foreclosed to satisfy some of these loans would not bring more than one-quarter or one-eighth of the principal invested. In the latter part of this month the premonitory indications of a fatal reaction began to appear. The direct exchanges between the city and the Eastern States had accumulated to a most important monthly aggregate, and a difficulty was beginning to manifest itself among parties called upon to make remittances. Each succeeding remittance made the difficulty greater, accommodations were more frequently asked, responses were made with reluctance, extraordinary negotiations were soon talked of, and finally an inundating distrust took possession of the public mind. Such a state of public feeling produced two difficulties so great, so overpowering in their nature that they were necessarily ruinous to men who chanced to be engaged in business which they did not sufficiently understand, with small capital, or with a large capital invested in real estate; and it must be remembered that at the time under consideration many of the business men of Sacramento were persons whose education and experience unfitted them for the positions they occupied. This was probably peculiarly the case with the principal banking houses in existence just prior to the heavy bankruptcies of August and September of this year. There were three regular banking establishments, and we question whether of the entire parties interested in them there was a single individual who was really competent in the business. This we say in no disrespect to the parties referred to but as a fact which goes very far to explain the sweeping revulsions experienced by them. The houses to which we refer were Barton Lee, Warbass & Co., and Hensley, McKnight & Hastings.

But banking was not the only business in which men were engaged that had not the necessary education and training to ensure success or to make success rationally probable. Men who had for years confined themselves to the tedious rounds of their particular business at the East regarded this as a good opportunity for changing their pursuits, and hence the unutterable compound of lawyers, doctors, ministers, merchants, mechanics, and laborers that in a few months became so entangled in the labyrinths of trade as to require a general train of rebuking bankruptcies to restore them to their senses and their legitimate callings.

Whilst public confidence continued to flood the city with the means of progress and the facilities of growing exchanges, nothing was easier than the management of business that was never subjected to any test of strength; but when the people engaged in developing the real resources of the state began not only to withhold expected supplies but to demand the return of those already furnished, then did the perils of the experimenters in business begin to appear. Then did this conglomerated mass begin a fermenting process which had no end but explosion, an explosion that shook Sacramento to its foundation. First in the terrible list of embarrassments was Barton Lee, who represented a capital of nearly a million and a half of dollars. Scarcely had the spirit of suspicion and conjecture accommodated him with embarrassments when his doors were closed, an assignment made, and the whole country paralyzed with panic-born attempts at collections.

In a few days Hensley, McKnight & Hastings suspended payments, and, shortly after, the house of Warbass & Co. followed the example of Lee and closed their doors with an assignment. A number of leading merchants followed the bankers, and in a few weeks the intoxicating progress of the city was arrested by a perfect *prostration* of confidence, an utter skepticism in the value of real estate, and a general excitability of the public mind as it vibrated between the ever changing points of hope and fear.

But Sacramento, that had outlived the antagonisms of Sutter, survived the general pauperism of the fall of '49, and reacted upon the floods of '50, was not only called upon now to undergo the lashings of a financial storm, but in the midst of all she was made the center of one of the most appalling riots that has been inflicted upon the country. We have reference to the squatter riots of the 15th of August, 1850.

At a period before referred to, an association of men known as squatters was formed in this city. The first meeting of that association was called by John H. Keyser at the house of a man by the name of Kelly, who kept a place of entertainment on Front Street above J. At this place meetings were frequently held prior to the flood. Sometimes these meetings would be very largely attended by men who came together from a variety of motives, as their conduct demonstrated.

The speakers at the meetings were at first not only entirely uneducated but so poorly sustained by native talent as to incur the ridicule of all but their immediate associates. But very soon men of talent and tact succeeded them and infused into their proceedings a degree of strength and popular pleadings that made the purchasers of Sutter titles watch their movements with anxiety. This anxiety was [increased] by an attention to the speaking squatters, for as a general thing their speeches were freighted with denunciations against "grasping and designing men," "speculators in lots and land monopolists." In the month of May the association was ably sustained by a most talented engineer, Col. Jno. Plumbe, [16]who was the regular surveyor and recorder of the organization. After the floods of January and March a more thorough and complete organization of this party took place, and a deep feeling of hostility sprang up between the squatters and the purchasers of Sutter titles. The members of the association began to demonstrate their views by settling upon lots in different parts of the town. Contests ensued and removals were being from time to time effected.

But on the 10th of May the particular suit was commenced which resulted in the riots of August; and to give a better conception of the character of this issue at law we must give a succinct record of the case.

On the 10th of May, 1850, Jno. P. Rodgers and Dewitt J. Burnett commenced action against Jno. T. Madden in the Recorder's Court, B. F. Washington presiding, under the statute providing for "unlawful entries and detainers." The lot settled upon and claimed Madden was situated on the southeast corner of N and Second streets. The case was sustained by Kewen and Morrison for the plaintiffs and F. W. Thayer for defendant. Defendant set forth a plea of no jurisdiction, issue joined, argued, and plea over-ruled. Defendant then instituted the plea of the property being public land, the freehold of the government of the United States, and therefore subject to a title by settlement and improvement—that about the first of March, 1850, he

---

[16] A pamphlet issued in March, 1850, by John Plumbe, presenting the squatters' view of the Sutter title, was reprinted by the Sacramento Book Collectors Club in 1942: *A Faithful Translation of the Papers Respecting the Grant Made by Governor Alvardo to John A. Sutter.*

had peaceably entered upon the premises and made improvements thereon. A demurrer was entered by plaintiffs upon the ground that the plea set forth by defendant was insufficient in law. The plea was overruled. The defendant then filed an affidavit asking a change of venue upon the ground that the recorder was biased and that he could not have fair trial in this city, the citizens also being prejudiced against him. The application was refused, and the case went to trial. The case being argued upon both sides, the recorder returned a judgment against defendant, fining him $300 and costs expended, and ordered the issuance of a writ of restitution.

The defendant appealed from this decision to the County Court, and on the 8th of August, 1850, the case came up for hearing before Judge Willis of the above tribunal. The defendant at this trial was assisted by McKune, Tweed, and Aldrich. Defendants moved for a nonsuit on the ground that the Recorder's Court had no jurisdiction over the case. The plea was taken into consideration, but by the consent of parties the case was submitted upon its merits. The claim of title from Sutter being offered by plaintiffs, defendant objected, and the objection was taken under advisement, which resulted in the court overruling the objection. The case was then argued, and the following day judgment was rendered sustaining the decision of the inferior court.

The defendant then asked to appeal to the Supreme Court, but there being no law at that time to sustain the appeal, the motion was overruled. During the proceedings of this trial both parties became excited to the utmost degree, and the squatters as a body declared against the restoration of the property pursuant to the judgments of the courts. Squatters and anti-squatters were holding meetings almost every night, and the town seemed full of wild excitement upon this question.

Almost immediately after the decision of Judge Willis was pronounced, the squatters issued the following poster:" [17]

"TO THE PEOPLE OF SACRAMENTO CITY.

"It is well known that a few individuals have seized upon nearly all the arable public lands in this county, and the following are some of the means they have resorted to in order to retain the property thus taken.

"First—They have used brute force and torn down the buildings of the settlers and driven them from their homes by riotous mobs.

"Second—They have used threats of violence, even to the taking of life, if the occupant or settler persisted in defending his property, and thus extorted from the timid their rightful possessions.

"Third—They have passed or procured the passage of certain rules in the so-called Legislature of California for the purpose, as their attorneys affirm, of protecting themselves and removing the settlers from the land they may occupy whether right or wrong— thus setting the question of title in an *assumed legislative* body, which question can alone be settled by the supreme government of the United States.

"Fourth—Under said legislative regulations, by them called they have continually harassed the settler with suits and in many instances compelled him to abandon his home for the want of the means to pay the costs of their courts. Many others have paid these costs with the hope of carrying their cause through these so-called courts to the proper tribunal for final decision, viz.—the Supreme Court of the United States.

"But these hopes were vain, for Judge Willis, so-called, has decided that from *his decision* there is *no appeal*

"And now, inasmuch as the so-called Legislature is not recognized by Congress, and their rules and regulations not approved and are therefore of no binding force upon the citizens of the United States but simply *advisory;* and inasmuch as the so-called law of 'Forcible Entry and Detainer,' if passed for the purpose affirmed by

---

[17] The manifesto of the squatters was also published in the Sacramento Transcript of August 12, 1850, p.3, col. 3.

their Council, namely to drive off settlers with or without title, is unconstitutional and would be in any state; the people in this community called settlers and others who are friends of justice and humanity, in consideration of the above have determined to disregard all decisions of our courts in land cases and all summonses or executions by the sheriff, constable, or other officer of the present county or city touching this matter. They will regard the said officers as private citizens, as in the eyes of the constitution they are, and hold them accountable accordingly. And, moreover, if there is no other appeal from Judge Willis, the settlers and others on the first show of violence to their persons or property, either by the sheriff or other person, under color of any execution or writ of restitution based on any judgment or decree of any court in this county in an action to recover possession of land, have *deliberately resolved to appeal to arms* and protect their sacred rights, if need be, with their lives.

"Should such be rendered necessary by the acts of the sheriff or others, the settlers will be governed by martial law. All property and the persons of such as do not engage in the contest will be sacredly regarded and protected by them, whether landholders or otherwise, but the property and lives of those who take the field against them will share the fate of war."

This card of the squatters increased the excitement in the community to such an intensity as to make collision and bloodshed an inevitable result in the premises. The card was pronounced to be a declaration of civil war and enlisted many people in the contest against the squatters who had previously favored them by a sort of passive approbation. On the 11th of August the squatters held a meeting upon the levee, which we find thus reported by the *Transcript* of August 12, 1850.[18]

---

[18] Sacramento *Transcript*, August 12, 1850, p. 2, col. 4. Morse corrected the original newspaper account in which the name of J. H. Mckune was erroneously spelled "McCune" and McClure." He also omitted twenty lines at the end containing a statement that the chairman of the meeting declared the resolutions were voted on and passed, but the editor believed the vote to have been equally divided.

"SQUATTER MEETING ON THE LEVEE.

"Resistance of Law Promulgated—Defense of Squatter? Rights
to Death—Intense Excitement.

"The meeting of the squatters at the foot of J Street on
Saturday evening was largely attended. The proceedings were
characterized by great excitement with a mixture of mirth and
sparkling wit which made the meeting decidedly 'rich and racy.' When
we arrived, Dr. Robinson, chairman of the meeting, was reading a
series of resolutions declarative of the sentiments of the squatters.
Among others was a resolution to resist decisions made by Judge
Willis of the County Court.

"A motion was adopted that the resolutions be taken up
separately. At this stage of the proceedings loud rails were made for
different speakers—'McKune, Kewen, Brannan, Barton Lee,
McClatchy &c.

"Mr. McKune appeared on the stand and had proceeded
about three quarters of an hour in an exposition of the Sutter tide and
defense of the squatters when he was interrupted by loud cries for 'a
new speaker,' 'Brannan, Kewen,' &c.

"The chairman at length succeeded in restoring order, assuring
the audience that Mr. Brannan should be heard when
Mr. McKune closed. During his speech, Mr. McK. made a statement
in regard to Mr. Sutter's place of residence, that if he had one any
more than another it was at Hock Farm and not at the fort, which was
promptly pronounced as 'false' by Mr. Brannan. This renewed the
commotion, and amidst a goodly sprinkling of noise and confusion Mr.
McKune had retired.

"The cries for different speakers were both loud and long. Mr.
Brannan and Judge Wilson took the stand. The latter stated he had just
returned to the city *with* a complete translation of the Mexican laws in
relation to land titles, and proceeded to show that the squatters were
vastly mistaken in regard to one or two of the arguments they use in
support of their rights and adverse to the validity of Capt. Sutter's title.

"Disorder again, reigned supreme until Mr. Brannan had
gotten fully under headway. Mr. B. proceeded to show that he was
justifiable in pronouncing the statement made by Mr. McKune as
being 'false, untrue.' Mr. B. also adverted to his agency in removing a
squatter from his land, 'land that had been paid for with money he had
earned by hard work.'

"Col. K J. C. Kewen was loudly called for. After considerable tumult, that gentleman took the stand and was proceeding when he was interrupted by cries of 'who's the speaker?' 'Give us your name? 'My name,' said Col. K., 'is Ed. Kewen, a man who is not afraid to face any populace or give expression to the honest convictions of his heart at any time or under any circumstances.' 'Are you a land holder?' Yes, I have a few acres of land which I have honestly acquired— and which I bought and paid for.' Col. K. remarked that many if those who were now here claiming land had been deluded by designing persons — that at heart they were honest men; and alluded to he general integrity of the Anglo-Saxon race. Whilst indulging-this strain, he was interrupted with cries of 'soft soap.' 'Yes,' replied the speaker, 'I believe there is a little too much *lie* in it, and I will forbear.' Col. K. referred to the decision of Judge Willis and controverted the position assumed by Mr. McKune. His remarks were received with plaudits on one side and disapprobation on the other.

"Dr. Robinson, the chairman, asked leave to address the meeting; at the same time Mr. Queen applied for a similar favor. Mr. Queen was denied the privilege, whereupon he turned to the assemblage and put the question for permission for the chair, which was also refused. (Roars of laughter.)

"Here there was a perfect war of words and bandying of set phrases between the squatters and others. The reading of the resolutions was loudly called for, when Dr. Robinson proceeded to read the first and then delivered a speech of considerable length in defense of the resolutions. Dr. R. closed with the remark that, as for himself, he meant to defend the property he had settled upon at all hazards...."

Madden retained possession of his premises for some time by the defense of members of the association. The house itself became a sort of garrison for the association, containing a variety of muskets, pistols, and some very antiquated sabers and swords. The sheriff, in his endeavors to execute the writ of restitution, discovered a number of individuals whom he knew among the party resisting his authority and reported the names of James McClatchy, Charles Robinson, and others, and warrants for their arrest were issued by Justice Sackett. The excitement continued to increase, and hasty and unwarrantable acts were committed on both sides for several days.

McClatchy had in the meantime delivered himself up and was confined in jail during the subsequent conflicts in the premises. Madden was finally dispossessed of his house but again recovered it on the 14th of August. On the morning and through the day of the 4th a crisis arrived which can be best appreciated by a republication of the incidents as then recorded by the journals.

(From the Daily Times of the 15th.) [19]
"YESTERDAY.

"At 2 o'clock a body of squatters, numbering about forty, proceeded to the foot of I Street on the levee and undertook to regain possession of a lot of ground which had been lately in the occupation of one of their party. They were fully armed, and a general understanding prevailed that their object included the liberation of the two men committed the day before to the prison ship upon the charge of being concerned in a riotous assemblage on the morning of the 12th for the purpose of forcibly resisting the process of law. After the displacement of some of the lumber upon the ground, the party of squatters were deterred from proceeding further in their intent. The mayor had meantime requested all good citizens to aid in suppressing the threatened riot, and very large numbers had gathered about the spot—several citizens, armed, proceeded also to the prison ship, but no demonstration was made in that direction.

"The squatters retreated in martial order and passed up I Street to Third, thence to J and up to Fourth, followed by a crowd of persons. They were here met by the mayor who ordered them to deliver up their arms and disperse. This they refused to do, and immediately several shots were fired at him, four of which took effect. He fell from his horse and was carried to his residence, dangerously if not mortally wounded. Mr. J. W. Woodland who, unarmed, stood near the mayor at the time, received a shot in the groin which he survived

---

[19] This issue of the *Placer Times* is not extant, and no comparison with the original could be made. Another contemporary account appears in the Sacramento *Transcript* of Aug 15, 1850, p. 2, col. 1-3

but a few moments. A man named Jesse Morgan, said to be from Millersville, Ohio, lately arrived, and who was seen to aim at the mayor, next fell dead from the effects of a ball which passed through his neck. Mr. James Harper was very severely but not dangerously wounded in supporting the sheriff. It is difficult to give an exact detail of the terrible incidents which followed in such rapid succession. It appeared from an examination before the coroner that the party of squatters drew up in regular order on arriving at the corner of Fourth Street, and that the sheriff was several times fired upon before he displayed any weapons. Testimony was also given as to the person who was seen to fire upon Mr. Woodland. The mounted leader of the squatters, an Irishman by the name of Maloney, had his horse shot under him; he endeavored to escape, was pursued a short distance up an alley and shot through the head, falling dead. Dr. Robinson, one of the armed party under his command, was wounded in the lower part of his body. Mr. Hale, of the firm of Crowell, Hale & Co., was slightly wounded in the leg. A young boy, son of Mr. Rogers, was also wounded. We have heard of several others but are not assured of the correctness of the reports. Upon the oath of several gentlemen that they saw Dr. Robinson deliberately aim at the mayor, he was arrested and placed in confinement. An Irishman named Caulfield, accused of a similar act with regard, to both the mayor and Mr. Woodland, was arrested late in the afternoon.

"After these terrible scenes, which occupied less time than we have employed to describe them, had passed, a meeting of the Council was held, the proceedings of which appear in another column. The citizens gathered at the corner of Second and J streets and other places throughout the city and proceeded to organize in parties to prevent further outrage. A body of mounted men under the command of the sheriff, hearing the report that the squatters were reinforcing at the fort, proceeded thither. The lawless mob was nowhere to be found; scouts were dispatched in all directions, but no trace of them could be discovered; meanwhile several other parties had formed into rank and proceeded to different parts of the city, establishing rendezvous at various points. Brigadier General Winn issued a proclamation declaring the city under martial law and ordering all law abiding citizens to form themselves into volunteer companies and report their organization at headquarters as soon as possible. At evening quiet was fully restored throughout the city. Lieut. Governor McDougal, who left upon the *Senator* and expects to meet the *Gold Hunter,* will bring up this morning a detachment of troops from Benicia. An extraordinary police force of 500 was summoned for duty during the night." By the minutes of the Council we find that B F Washington was appointed Marshal and Capt. J. Sherwood, assistant, to whom all persons desirous of making arrests were requested to apply for authority and aid. (From the Placer Times Extra of the 15th.)[20]

"LETTER FOUND IN THE TENT OF DR. ROBINSON- GENERAL STATE OF AFFAIRS—HEALTH AND CONDITION OF THE WOUNDED, ETC.

"The night passed without the least disturbance. The companies of Capt. Sherwood and Major Snyder and the artillery under Major Fowler were constantly on duty, also a police force of about - The greatest vigilance was observed, but no further arrests were made, and quiet seems to be fully restored throughout the city. The public mind is composed but resolute and fairly determined that the work shall be well done now. The few persons who were heard to promulgate opinions opposed to the action which the authorities have pursued have prudently desisted from their course, and but one sentiment is known at this time among the entire community. The squatters have successfully concealed themselves or fled. A proposition is very generally supported to give notice to all occupying city property as squatters to leave forthwith and that their tenements be demolished and all vestiges of their presence be removed. An early action to this direction will probably ensue. The most important development of the day is the letter found in the tent of Dr. Robinson and in his own handwriting, as can be fully proved. It is a damning evidence of the plans and purposes which governed the proceedings of the lawless mob of the 13th. We have no expression for the enormity of guilt which is thus brought home to them and all that abetted their cause.

"Lieut. Governor McDougal returned from Benicia on the *Gold Hunter* this morning, bringing fifty stand of arms and 1500 cartridges.

---

[20] No copy of this paper has been located. Robinson's letter also appeared in the Sacramento *Transcript* of August 16, 1850, p. 2. Col. 5.

NOTICE

TO

IMMIGRANTS!!

As there are in our City a number of men with remarkable principles, who go among those who have newly arrived and offer to sell or lease to them the *Public Land* in and about this place. thus imposing upon the unsuspecting. The latter are hereby notified that the vacant land in Sacramento City and vicinity. is open for *ALL*, free of charge ; but, they can make either of the following gentlemen a present of a few thousand dollars, if they have it to spare.. Such favors are eagerly sought and exultingly received by them. In fact. some of them are so solicitous in this matter. that. if they are not given *something*. they will *almost not like it*, and even threaten to *sue* people who will not contribute to their support. Those who have made themselves the most notorious, are

Barton Lee,	Prettyman, Barroll & Co.,	Warbass & Co.,
Burnett & Rogers,	A. M. Winn.	J. Sherwood,
Hardin Bigelow,	S. Brannan,	James Queen,
Pearson & Baker.	Hensley, Merrill & King,	Dr. W. G. Deal,
Thomas M'Dowell,	Conn. Mining and Trading Co.,	Eugene F. Gillespie,
R. J. Watson,	Paul, White & Co.,	T. L. Chapman,
J. S. Hambleton,	W M. Carpenter,	Dewey & Smith,
Starr, Bensley & Co.,	R. Gelston,	E. L. Brown,
	John S. Fowler.	

Sacramento City, June **14, 1850.**

"Sacramento Transcript" Print.

By order of the Settlers' Association.

NOTICE TO IMMIGRANTS

REPRODUCTION OF A BROADSIDE IN THE NEW YORK PUBLIC LIBRARY, ISSUED IN 1850 BY THE SACRAMENTO SETTLERS' ASSOCIATION.

"The arrangements for the funeral of Mr. J. W. Woodland are completed.

"A general expression of admiration is awarded to the conduct of the sheriff, Joseph McKinney. Under the most critical circumstances, bravery and discretion have united to commend his every action. He has been placed in positions demanding the exercise of the most exalted courage, and, in the midst of the most intense excitement which surrounded him, his perfect coolness and composure did not desert him To these attributes, as well as the fortune which favors the brave, is the preservation of his life owing; and our community may rejoice that such a well tried public officer continues to hold authority among men. He was during the melee the mark of many shots, but his vigilance and a kind Providence protected him

"We would allude in the same connection to the intrepid valor of Recorder Washington, upon whom the highest civic powers of command have devolved by the action of the Council with the enthusiastic and unanimous approbation of the entire community.

"Sheriff McKinney, on returning from the fort yesterday, entered the house of the surveyor of the Settlers' Association and took possession of all records, documents, &c., found therein."

"THE LETTER FOUND IN DR. ROBINSON'S TENT.

"August 12, 1850.—Although I have written one letter, yet, as I have been called upon by circumstances to remain in town, and as I have a little leisure, I will talk with you a little, my ever dear S.[21]" Since writing you we have seen much and experienced much of a serious and important character as well as much of excitement. The county judge before whom our cases were brought decided against us, and on Saturday morning declared that from his decisions there should be no appeal. The squatters immediately collected on the ground in dispute and posted on large bills the following: 'Outrage ! ! !—Shall Judge Willis be dictator? Squatters and all other republicans are invited to meet on the levee this evening to hear the details.' It was responded to by both parties, and the speculators, as aforetime, attempted to talk

---

[21] Sara T. D. Lawrence, who became Dr. Robinson's second wife on October 30, 1851, after his return east (See F. W. Blackmar. *The Life of Charles Robinson.* Topeka, Kansas, 1902)

104

against time, &c. On the passage of a series of resolutions presented by your humble servant, there were about three ayes to one nay, although the Transcript said they were about equal. Sunday morning I drew up a manifesto— carried it with me to the church—paid one dollar for preaching— helped them sing—showed it to a lawyer to see if my position was correct, legally, and procured the printing of it in handbills and in the paper[22] after presenting it to a private meeting of citizens for their approval, which I addressed at some length. After a long talk for the purpose of consoling a gentleman just in from the Plains, and who the day before had buried his wife whom he loved most tenderly, and a few days previous to that had lost his son, I threw myself upon my blankets and 'seriously thought of the morrow.'

"What will be the result? Shall I be borne out in my position? On whom can I depend? How many of those who are squatters will come out if there is a prospect of a fight? Will the sheriff take possession as he has promised before Io o'clock A. M.? How many speculators will fight? Have I distinctly defined our position in the bill? Will the world, the universe, and God say it is just? &c., &c., &c. Will you call me rash if I tell you that I took these steps to this point when I could get but 25 men to pledge themselves on paper to sustain me, and many of them, I felt, were timid? Such was the case.

"This morning I was early on my feet, silently and quietly visiting my friends, collecting arms, &c. Our manifesto appeared in the paper and in bills early, and the whole town is aroused. Nothing is thought or talked of but war. About 200 men assembled on the disputed territory, and most of them sympathized with us. A few, however, were spies. We chose our commander and enrolled such as were willing and ready to lay down their lives, if need be, in the cause. About 50 names could be obtained. I managed by speeches, business, &c., to keep the spectators and fighters mingled in a mass, all unarmed, so as to let no one know but all were men of valor and ready to fight. While thus engaged, the mayor appeared and addressed us from his saddle—not *ordering* us to disperse but *advising* us to do so. I replied most respectfully that we were assembled to injure no one and to assail no one who left us alone. We were on our own property with no hostile intentions while unmolested. After he left, I, with others, was

---

[22] The manifesto already quoted by Morse above, p. 73-75, and printed in th Sacramento Transcript of August 12, 1850, p. 3, col. 3

appointed a committee to wait upon him at his office and state distinctly our positions, &c., so that there could be no possibility of mistake. He said he should use his influence as an individual to keep anyone from destroying our property and told us the sheriff had just told him that the executions from the court had been postponed. We returned and, after reporting and making some further arrangements for another meeting if necessary, we adjourned. I told the mayor we should not remain together if no attempt was to be made to execute their warrants, but I told him if in the meantime a sheriff or any other person molested a squatter, we should hold him responsible according to our proclamation. From this position we could not be driven although we knew it was in violation of die regulations of the state. We were prepared to abide the result.

"It is said that a writ is made out for my arrest as a rebel, &c. If so, it will not probably be served at present."

(From the *Daily Times* of the 16th.)[23]

"Another day of gloom arrives in the dread succession which we are compelled to record. Scarcely had the funeral rites been rendered to one victim ere a second is immolated upon the sacred altar of duty. The sheriff of this county, Joseph McKinney, was killed last evening. He had proceeded to Brighton in company with a party of about twenty to make arrests of persons whom he had been advised were concerned in the riotous outrages of the 14th. On reaching the pavilion and being assured that the parties sought for were at the hotel of one Allen in the neighborhood, it was arranged that Mr. McDowell of Mormon Island, well known at the house, should proceed there, make observations and return. They did not wait for him, however, but soon after rode up to the door when the sheriff demanded of Allen that he and the others should surrender themselves. They refused to do this, and immediately several shots were fired, mortally wounding Mr. McKinney. He expired in a few moments. Meanwhile, several of those with him had entered the bar room where about a dozen squatters were assembled. Three of the latter were killed on the

---

[23] No copy of the Sacramento Placer Times of August 16, 1850, is available. Another conptmporary account is found in the Sacramento Transcriot of August 16, 1850, p. 2, col. 1-2

spot. Allen escaped, though wounded. Three prisoners were taken and brought into town. We have heard that a fourth and a negro squatter were also taken.

"At the time the first report of these proceedings reached the city, the Council was in session. Messrs. Tweed and Spalding were appointed to unite with Capt. Sherwood in taking measures to meet the emergency. Numbers of the citizens left immediately for the scene of disturbance. The greatest commotion pervaded the city and the most contradictory and exaggerated rumors were circulated. It was feared that in the excitement the protection of the city would be neglected. In the course of a few hours the facts became known and quiet was restored. Messengers continued to arrive throughout the night. A strict patrol was kept in the vicinity of Brighton and of this city. A man *was* arrested by Capt. Sherwood, being identified by two or three persons as implicated in the riot of the 14th. We are denied room for comment. But a few hours ago we had the satisfaction to give a just tribute of appreciation to the gallant conduct of the officer whose sacrifice we now relate Every member of our community feels in his own person the enormity of the crime which has been committed against all the social and political rights prized by our countrymen. A similar outrage is almost unprecedented in the history of the American people, and every interest of this community demands that the retribution should be summary and complete."

The following is the dispatch sent to Gen. Winn by Governor Burnett when he heard of the troubles at Sacramento:

"SAN JOSE, August 15, 1850.

"To Brig. Gen. A. M Winn, Second Brigade, First Division, California Militia :

"Sir: It having been made to appear to me that there is a riotous and unlawful assembly with intent to commit a felony at Sacramento City, in Sacramento County, you will forthwith order out the whole of your command to appear at Sacramento City on the 16th day of August, 1850, or as soon thereafter as practicable; and you will take command of the same and give all the aid in your power to the civil authorities in suppressing violence and enforcing the laws. Should the force ordered out not be sufficient, you will forthwith inform me accordingly.

"Your obedient servant, Peter H. Burnett,
"Governor of California and Commander-in-Chief."

On the morning of the 16th two military companies arrived by the steamer *Senator* from San Francisco under command of Captains Howard and McCormick, accompanied by Col. J. W. Geary, Mayor, who placed themselves under command of Gen Winn, who transmitted to the Common Council the following letter:

"BRIGADE HEADQUARTERS, August I 7, 1850.

"To the Acting Mayor and Common Council
    of Sacramento City:

"I have the honor to inform you that the Second Brigade, First Division, California Militia, is now in readiness to give aid to the civil authorities in supressing violance and enforcing law.
"Any orders emanating from your board shall be promptly attended to.

"With high respect, I subscribe myself your obedient servant,
                              "A. M. WINN, Brig. Gen.
                                   "By E. J.C. KEWEN,
            "Asst. Adj. Gen., 2d Brig., Ist Div., California Militia.

The Council then made the following reply :

"Council Chamber, Sacramento City, August 17, 1850.

"Sir: Your communication of this date is received, notifying me of the readiness of the Second Brigade, First Division, California Militia, under your command, to aid the civil authorities in suppressing violence and enforcing law, and stating that any orders emanating from this board shall be promptly attended to. In reply I would state

108

that immediately after the unexpected riot of the 14th instant a police force of five hundred men was authorized to be raised and B. F. Washington, Esq., appointed as marshal to take command, aided by Capt. J. Sherwood.

"Thus far this force has proven itself capable of sustaining our laws and protecting the property of our citizens without resort to military aid, and from all the information which we now possess there is no great probability of such aid being needed.

"Should any emergency arise requiring it, rest assured we shall avail ourselves of your kind offer.

"By order of the board,

D. STRONG,
"President of the Common Council and Acting Mayor."

"PROCLAMATION.

"FELLOW CITIZENS Peace, order, and quietness have re-assumed their sway. Scouts have returned after scouring the neighborhood and report the absence of any appearance of hostilities. A heavy guard is constantly maintained and the city is safe from an attack. Reliable information has been received from the mines, assuring us of the falsity of the rumors of assemblages to resist the law. An observance of the ordinance against discharging fire arms in the city is commanded. Especially is it necessary at this time after nightfall. Officers on duty will attend to this. No further disturbance is apprehended, but our vigilance must not be relaxed.

"D. STRONG,
"President of Common Council and Acting Mayor.
"August 19, 1850."

(From the Transcript of August 19th.)

"RESTORING OF QUIET.

"We are happy to see at last the dawning of a calmer state of things in our midst. Under the circumstances, the excitement of the past few days was perhaps unavoidable. It is a terrible step for men to take to rise in armed opposition to the laws and constitution of the state in which they reside. But when such a step is taken it must be promptly met.

"Our citizens have aroused with determination; they have rushed in multitudes to the side of law and authority. The blow has been struck. The armed opposition has been crushed. The rioters are scattered, and the authority of our government is still maintained. In addition, two telling moral blows have been struck whose effect will last long in our community. We allude to the funerals of Mr. Woodland and of Mr. McKinney. It almost seemed as if the entire city rose to perform over them the last duties which were left to be performed.

"At present all is quiet in our midst. And we trust that until there is need of further excitement, our fellow citizens will do what lies in their power to allay the turmoil which has jostled our city from its course of prosperity.

"The remote evils resulting from such an excitement as we have passed through are much to be deplored and should be avoided if it is within the range of possibility. The utter stagnation of all business, the cessation of works of public improvement, the stop placed upon private works of enterprise, the forgetfulness of the thousand and one subjects which should demand the immediate attention of the public, these all call upon us to allay the excitement no longer called for and to resume our former condition of quiet."

The death of Capt. Woodland was the result of an exposure that was prompted by one of the noblest impulses of the human heart. He was walking up the street and near the corner of J and Fourth in company with a friend of ours when the squatters ranged themselves diagonally across Fourth with their guns presented towards the approaching mayor and his party. The moment he saw the menacing attitude of these men he exclaimed to this individual, "Oh it's too bad for these men to take such a stand, for they will certainly be shot down, and I will go up and advise them." In an attempt to execute this intention he stepped forward but a couple of steps when he received a ball that killed him almost instantly.

After Mayor Bigelow had been disabled by his wounds received on the 14th, Demas Strong became the acting mayor for the balance of Bigelow's term. He was formerly president of the Council.

Up to the 6th of August the amount of $100,000 had been issued per warrants to meet expenditures of city government as shown by the mayor's statement, and the estimated expense to be incurred by the construction of the levee and city government inclusive presented a sum total of $300,000.

No pen could describe the trouble which Sacramento endured during this and the succeeding month. The contests about titles, the breaking up of confidence in the general value of property thus situated, the pecuniary embarrassments that were running men into bankruptcy and ruin, and the heavy taxation necessary to sustain the city government and complete the public works which were necessary to the protection of the city from floods, were enough to drive the city into an irrecoverable destruction; but the city had been established by a community of men of iron wills and inextinguishable energy. It could not be destroyed, as has been shown in a manner that leaves no room for doubt upon the subject. We have nearly omitted to mention an act of the Council, we believe in August, by which they appropriated to themselves a salary of $200 each a month. This was a most unpopular movement, and when, in addition to this, the citizens saw committees authorized by the Council attending to duties that were little more than nominal and receiving for their services $25 per day in addition to the monthly appropriation, there was a high degree of dissatisfaction engendered.

After the riots of August, squatterism seemed for a time totally dead so far as squatting upon city property was concerned, and after the bankruptcies of September the people began more systematically and much *more* soundly to engage in business, which was made extraordinarily good by the heavy transportation of merchandise to the mines. The winter previous, the people in the mines were thrown into desperate and starving condition from the scarcity of provisions and the interruption of communication with the city. Hence this fall, soon after the financial revulsion, an immense and profitable trade sprang up between merchants and miners. This was a most timely relief and exerted such a magic effect upon the city in a few weeks as to almost reestablish all its former indications of prosperity.

A public question then of great interest began to occupy the minds of men and cause them to watch every successive arrival from Washington with the most intense anxiety. We mean the question of admission *as* a state into the Union. The long delay of Congress to acknowledge us as a state had induced a most painful suspense. Under such circumstances it can easily be imagined how the information was received, when it did come, that California had taken her stand as one of the commonwealths of the Federal Union.

Early in the morning of the 15th of October (we believe)"[24]

---

[24] The news of the admission of California reached Sacramento about 3:30 A. M., October 21, 1850, with the arrival of the steamer *New World.* (Sacramento Transcript, Oct. 21, 1850, p. 2, col. 2.) It had been received at San Francisco the previous morning on the Oregon.

112

the booming notes of a rapidly fired cannon upon the levee waked the citizens of Sacramento with the understood and emphatic assurances of *admission.* The sun rose that morning upon a community of people so elated with joyful intelligence, so intoxicated with the dissipation of an oppressive suspense, that every memory from that terrible past seemed to be blotted from their recollection. In addition to the agreeable and exciting information, there were a great many of our old citizens returning by the same steamer that brought the news.

But, alas, the exuberance of spirit thus enkindled, the joyous and buoyant feelings thus excited, were but the illusive precedents of one of the most appalling calamities that had ever yet set its seal of distress upon the destiny of the Valley City. Associated with the glorious intelligence of our admission into the great confederation. The news of the admission of California reached Sacramento about 3:3o A. M., October 19, 1850, with the arrival of the steamer *New World.* (Sacramento *Transcript,* Oct. 21, 1850, p. 2, col. 2.) It had been received at San Francisco the previous morning on the f states was the sad assurance that a most malignant cholera was weeping on towards California, and that the passengers on the very steamer that brought the news had many of them fallen victims a this terrific scourge.

Every successive day brought intelligence from the Bay that the newly arrived passengers were still dying with cholera. These evidences of its appearance upon the shores of California and the heartrending accounts of the disease as it was visiting Rochester, Sandusky, and St. Louis, created such a dread of its approach, such in inexpressible fear of the destruction which marked its progress,) if the malignant and hopeless rapidity with which it hurried its victims into eternity, that the people watched its manifestations with in excitability

113

of mind that can seldom be induced by any scene) earth. It is doubtful whether in the records of the world there could be found a parallel of the destructive panic which followed his appearance of cholera in our midst. Previous difficulties from which our citizens had but just escaped and which were sufficient to rush any ordinary energy, and the short interval afforded them for recuperating, made them the easy prey of disease and death.

In the feverish state of mind that existed in the community there was no hope of escape. This alone, with the direction then given :o fears, was sufficient to coerce the disease into a terrific development. It scarcely required an imported case to establish a panic more to be dreaded than its cause, the cholera. But we believe the first case that occurred was a steerage immigrant of the steamer which brought this disease. Early on the morning of the 20th of October a person was found on the levee in the collapsing stage of this formidable malady. Medical aid was administered, but the disease had taken too deep hold of its victim. We saw him at sunrise. He was then expiring from the effects of the disease. The indications presented by his death were not calculated to abridge the depressing fear in the community. The cholera was now indeed in our city, and from mouth to mouth the story was communicated, so improved in all the features of a horrible description as to darken the city with the very pall of death in a few hours. Time and Mortality, discovering the advantages conceded to them by the panic-stricken community, did not lose the opportunity of commencing the work of destruction. The next day several fatal cases were duly chronicled and as duly circulated through the magnifying minds of thousands of individuals whose fear of the disease made them the almost certain subjects of it. With such assistance any disease of common severity might have decimated the city, and hence it was not at all singular that cholera should have become a terrible destroyer.

In six days from the time of its inception it was making such progress that regular burials were but slightly attended to, and nursing and attention were not unfrequently functions of society that were entirely overlooked. Money would scarcely buy the offices of common kindness, and affections were so neutralized by the conflicting elements of selfishness that but little could be done to arrest the course of the disease.

The victims of the malady did not seem to be confined so much to those of intemperate and irregular habits as had been the case in almost all the previous manifestations of the disease. People of the most industrious, regular, and careful habits seemed alike vulnerable to the dreadful enemy. In a few days many of our most substantial citizens were numbered among the victims to the sweeping epidemic. It was reported that a hundred and fifty cases occurred in a single day; but such was the confusion and the positive delirium of the community that no proper records were made, nor can any accurate data now be found in respect to this epidemic of '50. As soon, however, as the daily mortality became so great as to keep men constantly employed in carrying away the dead, the citizens began to leave the town in every direction and in such numbers as to soon diminish the population to probably not more than one-fifth of its ordinary standard. In this pestilential reign of terror and dismay the most dreadful abandonments of relatives and friends took place. Those who were willing to forget self and become the visitants of mercy constituted but a small and meager proportion of the many who, following the instincts of nature, sought only to preserve themselves. There were a few men, as there always will be, whose history of warm hearts throbbed with an uncontrollable anxiety to convey relief to the distressed and the dying, men who lingered around the death scenes of the epidemic so spellbound by sympathy that they endured anything and everything as long as there remained a solitary hope of even palliating the agony of dissolving nature. Such men there were engaged in the noble task of delineating the only real divinity of man during this terrible slaughter scene of 1850—men who were drawn to the appalling scenes of human misery, then developed, as irresistibly as the magnetic needle bends to the mysterious attractions of the north. These men are found by and are known to those who constitute the heroes of all epidemics. They consisted of an occasional brother whose inwrought feelings of fraternity were sustained by a maternal bias that made them as enduring as life and as constant as the altar fires of Eternal Truth, by fathers, uncles, cousins, or friends, in whose companionship circulated the deathless elements of enduring, immortal affections.

But in a constricted and hurried sketch like this there is no space for the incorporation of names that are written in the pages of individual memories and, as we believe, recorded in the indestructible roll of Heaven's favorites. But we will mention one name, our motive for which will be readily acknowledged more as the extortion of truth than the result of partisan partiality. That name is John Bigler, the present Governor of California. This man, with strong impulses of sympathy, could be seen in every refuge of distress that concealed the miseries of the dying and the destitute. With a lump of gum camphor as large as a moderate sized inkstand, now in his pocket and anon at his nostrils, he braved every scene of danger that presented, and with his own hands administered relief to his suffering and uncared-for fellow beings. Nothing could have absorbed such an amount of confidence in any man's mind as did this huge piece of camphor in the feelings of Col. Bigler; and the involuntary industry with which he applied it to the olfactory avenues of sensation gave to the habit such a ludicrous appearance as to almost provoke an unhallowed smile amidst the most solemn scenes that can pass the portals of vision. With a little transposition it seemed to be the very embodiment of a portion of Cato's soliloquy, in which he says—

"Thus am I doubly armed,
My death and life, my bane and antidote, are both before me;
This (the cholera) in a moment shall bring me to an end,
But this (the camphor) informs me I shall not die."

But no rational source of protection, no means of relieving the mind from an instinctive fear that depresses the vital forces, should ever disparage those ennobling impulses of benevolence which conduct a man voluntarily into the haunts of danger and distress. They may at times appear in a ridiculous light, but they are honorable, just, and in the highest degree serviceable. If their general application could impart a similar feeling of safety, the cholera would become a disease of so much tameness as to make it nearly as amenable to remedies as are the intermittents of our country.

But we imagine we hear the interrogative exclamation of "who are the heroes of epidemics?" Well, suppose we answer that they are the faithful and educated physicians of all countries who rush with unfaltering determination and a total forgetfulness of self into the thickest dangers that malignant disease can possibly evolve. Is there an objection to the panegyric? Is it too liberal a compliment for the self-enshrinement of the faculty? Popularly it may be, but by the hands of an invisible biographer it is a tribute of justice so recorded as to be of more service than all the patronage of a fleeting commendation. It is a sacred and sublime truth for which the physician endures an infinite variety of dangers in time that in eternity he may hold it as an endless source of agreeable contemplation.

Never, never did the faculty exhibit a more noble, daring, and beautiful courage than in this, the worst trial scene of firmness to which the profession was probably ever subjected in the world. The rapid spreading of the epidemic gave to the physicians of the city no rest, day or night. Did they sink for a time under the pressure of exhausted strength and determine to take a few moments for restoring themselves, they were roused again by the earnest and imploring messages for relief that penetrated every barrier to disturbance that they might erect. As might be expected, they were falling like the foremost soldiers of a desperate charge, and ere this cholera season had subsided *seventeen* of their number were deposited in the sandhill cemetery of our city. A professional mortality never known—an inroad of death from which but a fraction more than two in three escaped with life, and not one in three from the disease. And yet not a single educated physician turned his back upon the city in its distress and threatened destruction. More we could say without a blush of inconvenience or the least reproach from an inconsistent violation of professional modesty.

This awful calamity lasted in its malignant form but about twenty days, but by the unsystematic records of the times the number of deaths cannot be ascertained. Besides those who died in the city, many were overtaken by death in other places and upon the road, in the desperate efforts of our citizens to escape by running from the enemy. In the latter part of the epidemic the authorities, that had from the first been most constant in their efforts at relief, procured the use of a large frame building in L Street where the destitute cholera subjects were taken and well provided for.

The abatement of the disease was much longer than its period of inception and increase and commenced just as soon as the frequency of death had familiarized people with the frightful scenes around them and rendered them less defenseless from a paralyzing and destructive fear.

By the time that the disease had almost completely disappeared, the city was nearly depopulated, and there were not a few outside croakers on destiny that intimated that the Levee City was dead beyond a possibility of resurrection.

But those who supposed Sacramento and Sacramentans could be so easily crushed had not learned their character. The very moment that mortality began an obvious retreat from our premises, that very moment those who survived their flight returned, and those who abided by the city in its distress reacted upon the calamities of the town with such an elastic and vigorous energy as to completely transform the appearance of the place in a few days. The confidence of the people in the health of the city was almost immediately restored, and business communications were re-opened with the mines under the most encouraging circumstances. For a few weeks a good business was realized, and the broken and beautiful winter that followed imparted a vitality to the town that could not have been anticipated by one who contemplated its destiny through the gloomy scenes of the

October previous.

Merchants and traders had unfortunately calculated too much upon a winter like that of '48 and '49 in which the communication with the mines was for a long time suspended. This induced them to transport at high rates immense stores into different mining regions, which stores in consequence of the lack of water in dry diggings and the uninterrupted communication with the city this following winter were sold at ruinous sacrifices.

Never was any portion of the world so blest by the comforts of a sunny and almost unclouded winter as California during this season. Everything that belongs to a balmy air, a beautiful horizon, and unexceptionable temperature was experienced in this nominal winter, but real Indian summer. And although it brought not so much of the glittering ore into our city, yet it poured into the golden treasury of health such elements of future growth and power, such sources of gratitude and motives to contentment that all men seemed to be happy.

The winter passed away almost unnoticed, save by its genial influences, and never were realized more delightful comminglings of business and pleasure. Such an introduction as was given to 1851 can find no parallel in history, and it seems almost impossible that its counterpart can ever appear in the future. But we cannot begin to do justice to the balance of our city's existence and progress unless awarded more time and space and infinitely less of the impetuous hurry which has forced us through what we have already accomplished. From the spring of '51 the following prominent records (taken from the files of the *Union*) are predicated upon a promise of future opportunity to better arrange and introduce them for a separate and specific edition of the *History* [25] itself.

April 5th, [1851]. The Sacramento River reported higher than at any previous date of the season. Green peas in market.

April 15th. City divided into wards.

April 29th. *Union* became a party paper.

May 1st. First mail left for Salt Lake.

May 5th. Municipal election held, at which 2,482 votes were cast, and Jas. R. Hardenbergh, elected Mayor; W. H. McGrew, Recorder;}. Neely Johnson, City Attorney; W. S. White, Marshal and Collector; W. R. McCracken, Treasurer; S. F. McKee, Assessor; John Requa, Harbor Master; and Messrs. Jos. A. Haines, R. Chenery, Richard, B. F. Johnson, Carey Peebles, E. D. Kennedy, Addison Martin, C. I. Hutchinson, L. B. Patchin, and Dr. Duncombe, Councilmen; L. Curtis, Clerk.

By report of treasurer the receipts of the fiscal year ending May 6th were $214,939.86.

The mayor's message, May 12th, shows the indebtedness to be $368,551.29, $80,000 of which was drawing from 10 to 20 per cent per month interest, the balance from 3 to 8 per cent per month.

June. Council passed an ordinance funding city debt at to per cent interest per year, payable in New York, and 12 Per cent Per Year> payable in Sacramento.

July 4th. Grand celebration of the Declaration of Independence by the different associations of the city, upon which occasion Murray Morrison read the Declaration of Independence and B. D. Fry delivered an oration in the Rev. Mr. Benton's church.

---

[25] Dr. Morse's more complete history of Sacramento never materialized. For a fuller statement regarding the proposed work see the preface to this book.

August 13th. Tehama Theater burned.

September.' Popular vote of the county, 4,115.

September 9th. American Theater erected and opened by Dr. Volney Spalding.

December 24th. Court house finished.

December 30th. Sacramento River up within four feet of its natural banks.

January 10th, 1852. *Union* issued its first weekly.

January 14th. State offices and legislature removed to Sacramento. First session, January 16th.

January 16th. Ball given at the Orleans Hotel in honor of state officers.

January 20th. 1,000 persons per steamboat arrived in one day.

January 23d. Brick row on K Street commenced.

February 5th. The *Democratic State Journal* issued its first number, published and edited by Geiger & Co.

February 9th. N. A. H. Ball appointed by the Common Council, City Treasurer, in place of McCracken, absent.

March 7th. City overflowed; water first broke the flood gate of Sutter Lake.

April 5th. Municipal election held at which 2,802 votes were cast. C. I. Hutchinson elected Mayor; W. H. McGrew, Recorder; R. Chenery, Treasurer; G. Hyer, City Attorney; John Requa, Harbor Master; D. McDowell, Marshal and Collector; Wm. Lewis, Assessor; J. A. Haines, C. W. Barker, S. C. Fogus, Wm. H. Watson, J. H. Nevett, J. Forshee, G. W. Chedic, T. P. Robb, and J. H. Updgraff , Councilmen—all Whigs. By the mayor's message of this year the indebtedness stands at $449,105.32; estimated revenue of the incoming year, $200,000.

June 7th. Whig state convention met in Sacramento for the purpose of electing delegates to the national convention. The *Times and Transcript* removed to San Francisco.

June 14th. Board of Supervisors for the county elected.

June 27th. Sutter Light Infantry, a rifle corps, organized ; B. D. Fry, Captain; M. D. q1, First Lieut.

July 1st. Citizens in every part of the city busily engaged in making improvements; most prominent in the city were the new buildings of J. P. Overton.

July 4th. Marysville Hook and Ladder Company entertained by Mutual Hook and Ladder Company No. 1 of this city.

July 5th. National independence celebrated in a style surpassing in grandeur every other exhibition in the city; upon this occasion D. J. Lisle read the Declaration of Independence, and M. S. Latham delivered an oration.

July 17th. Election held, when the people voted for the construction of a wide levee through I Street and *also* the erection of a city hall and prison.

August 2d. R. M. Folger elected Chief Engineer of the Fire Department.

August 12th. Henry Clay's obsequies celebrated; processions marched through the streets; houses draped in mourning, and eulogy delivered by Hon. Tod Robinson.

September 6th. Peaches first in market, price 25 and 50 cents each. About this time a large amount of stock arrived in the city from across the Plains.

September 27th. Alert Hook and Ladder Company No. 2 organized

October 7th. Proposition made to Common Council to light the city with gas.

October 8th. Agricultural fair by J. L. L. F. Warren; at its close an address on agriculture was delivered by Dr. John F. Morse. Population of the city at this date between eleven and twelve thousand souls.

November 2d. Awful conflagration.

November 13th. Mayor presented a message showing an additional tax necessary.

November 17th. *Californian*"[26]issued first number.

December 9th. In accordance with resolutions of the citizens and Common Council,. W. Winans delivered a eulogy upon Daniel Webster.

December 17th. Terrible storm of four days duration, rivers rising with great rapidity and threatening to flood the city.

December 25th. Upper part of the city flooded.

January 1st, 1853. Totally submerged and water higher than ever known. A day of unusual hilarity and sport.

January 13th. People voted for water works, fire department, loan, and three-quarters per cent additional taxation. In this month many mercantile houses established branches of their business at Hoboken. Trade entirely cut off from the city on account of the high water and impassable condition of the road.

---

[26] Of the several publications having the title *Californian*, this was the Sacramento morning newspaper which presented the political views of the settler Democrats. It fused with the *Democratic State Journal* on the following July 30th. ([E. C. Kemble] *A History of the California Newspapers* . . . Reprinted for the *First Time form the Sacramento Daily Union of December 25, 1858*, New York, 1927, p. 159 – 160.

April 5th. Municipal election held and officers elected as appears in appendix of general information.[27]

The mayor's message this year gives no financial statement.

But even in the Directory edition we cannot forbear a concluding reference to the gigantic improvements which are now

---

[27] The list of city officials which appeared in the appendix to the 1853 city directory is as follows:

City officers elected the 4th day of April, 1853, and whose term of office will expire on the 4th day of April, 1854.

Mayor—J. R. Hardenbergh, office, 48 K Street.
Recorder—N. Greene Curtis, Court Room, 48 K Street.
Common Council—First Ward: R. P. Johnson, P. J. Hickey,* J. T. Moore. Second Ward: P. H. Burnett, R. A. Pearis, John Gillig. Third Ward: Samuel Youngs, C. H. Bradford, A. S. Gove. Secretary of Common Council, John A. Fowler. Chamber, 48 K Street.
    Standing Committees—Finance: Messrs. Pearis, Bradford, Moore. Streets and Public Places: Youngs, Pearis, Johnson. Applications for Office: Gillig, Gove, Hickey. Police and Watch: Gove, Moore, Hickey. Hospital and Sick: Bradford, Pearis, Johnson. Contracts and Expenditures: Burnett, Hickey, Moore. Printing: Burnett, Moore, Bradford. Nuisances: Hickey, Gillig, Bradford. Fire and Water: Gove, Gillig, Johnson. Levee: Burnett, Pearis, Johnson. Ways and Means: Burnett, Hickey, Johnson. Special Committee on Permanent Improvement of the Streets: Burnett, Bradford, Moore.
    Attorney—Lewis Sanders, Jr., office, Read's Building.
    Treasurer—C. J. Torbert, office, corner J and Fourth.
    Marshal and Collector—William S. White, office, 48 K Street. Deputy Marshal—Lambert Welborn.
    Deputy Collector of Licenses and Taxes—M. D. Corse, office, 48 K Street.
    Assessor—S. T. Clymer.
    Harbor Master—G. Backus, office, storeship Dimon.
    City Surveyor—C. W. Coote, office, 48 K Street.
    City Physician—J. F. Montgomery, office, 81 J Street.
    Captain of Police—John McClory, office, Station House.
    Lieutenant of Police—R. P. Jacobs, office, Station House.
    Commissioners of Funded Debt—J. R. Hardenbergh, ex officio; D. O. Mills; S. H. Meeker; C. J. Torbert, ex officio Secretary; D. O. Mills, Treasurer.
                    *P. J. Hickey resigned

going on in our wonderful city.

The levee on the Sacramento and American rivers is being rapidly widened and raised; a new levee from the former to the highlands in the rear of the city is in course of construction; the raising of I Street to a level above high water mark and the extension of that improvement to Tenth Street, all of which will be completed within a few weeks, will effectually secure the city against a recurrence of the calamity from which she has so frequently and so terribly suffered. The planking of Front Street from I to M Street, K Street from Front to Eighth, Second Street from J to K, and J Street from Front to Twelfth, where it connects with the plank road to Patterson's (12 miles), is progressing rapidly and will all be completed before the wet season.

Thus the city, secure from flood and accessible at all times by its main artery of internal trade, with every facility for rapid communication between its different quarters secured by the planking of the principal thoroughfares, would seem to require but protection against fire to be insured a career of future prosperity. A repetition of the frightful conflagration of last November has been effectually guarded against by the construction since that time of over two hundred fireproof brick structures, most of which from their massive walls and metallic defenses bid defiance to eternal attacks of the devouring element.

Among the most prominent buildings commanding our admiration from the solidity of their construction and architectural proportions, we would mention the granite front building of the celebrated house of Adams & Co. The granite used in its construction has been taken from a quarry about so miles from this city and at great expense prepared for this building, the first in which California granite has been used and which will vie favorably with any that the world can produce. This building is 36 x 75 feet, three stories high, so elegant in its massive construction, so thoroughly fireproof and perfect in all its parts that it surpasses all previous efforts at grandeur and fully sustains the reputation of Adams & Co. for advancement and indefatigable enterprise. With this building we would mention the extensive pile of Read & Co., 60 x 160, corner of Third and J streets; Orleans Hotel; Callahan's Hotel, K Street; Kennedy's building, corner of Third and J streets; John Gillig's store, J Street; H. E. Robinson's, J Street; Spalding & Johnson's new building, the Magnolia; K Street row, between Second and Third; Mineral Point Hotel on J Street; Boyd & Davis on K Street; J. Beam, and Cothrin & PotterCou, on K Street above Third; Brown, Henry & Co., T. S. Mitchell & Co., S. D. Jones & Co., and D. O. Mills & Co. on J Street, besides numerous stores and buildings in different parts of the city equally worthy of note but too numerous to mention in detail. We only desire to name the immense building now in course of erection on Front Street by Dr. Carpenter. This house is 80 x 85 feet, three stories in height. The beautiful location of this structure and its immense size commend it as a suitable building for the state capitol if, as is generally supposed, the legislature remove here the coming winter. It would afford ample accommodations for both houses, their committee and officers' rooms, the executive departments, governor, etc., thus adding materially to the general convenience of all interested.

The fire department will in a short time receive an ample

supply of efficient apparatus which has been sent for to the Atlantic cities. Capacious cisterns have been provided in different localities; extensive water works have been contracted for and are in course of construction—the pipes being all on the ground, there is a reasonable probability that they will be in operation at an early date. With these improvements and precautions the prosperity of the city is secured: its future is no longer a doubt, but a certainty—Sacramento must continue to be the SECOND CITY OF CALIFORNIA.

HISTORICAL SKETCH, 1851

By J. Horace Culver[28]

TOPOGRAPHY

---

[28] This historical sketch of Sacramento is reprinted here chiefly because of its antiquarian interest as accompanying the first published directory of the town: *The Sacramento City Directory. By J. Horace Culver. January z, z851.* (Sacramento City, Transcript Press, 1851, p. 71-83.) Compiled from personal observation and hearsay evidence, it includes many interesting historical facts and a few misstatements. John A. Sutter arrived at the site of Sacramento in August, 1839, not in March, and Marshall's gold discovery was made in January, not in February, 1848. The survey of the town by William H. Warner *was* begun in December, 1848, and there is some dispute concerning who erected the first building in the city. No attempt has been made to correct minute inaccuracies.

James Horace Culver, who compiled and published the *Sacramento City Directory* of 1851, went to Volcano in Amador (then Calaveras) County before coming to Sacramento, and he was there elected alcalde of the district in September, 1849. At Sacramento in April, 1850, he became one of the firm of Ormsby, Culver & Company, real estate agents, and acted at the same time as an auctioneer. He published the first city directory on January 1, 185x, including the historical sketch here reprinted. In February, 1851, Culver became the proprietor of the Missouri Hotel on J Street and in June of the next year entered the lime and cement business, in which he continued until his death. He died on May 11, 1864, at the age of fifty-one and was buried in the Masonic plot, City Cemetery, Sacramento. He was survived by his wife, the former Kate M. Penny, whom he had married on May 26, 1858. *(Colville's Sacramento Directory,* 1856, P. 37; *San Francisco Herald,* May 29, 1858, P. 3, col. 4; Sacramento *Union, May* 12, 1864, p. 3, col. r, and May 16, 1864, p. 3, col. 2; vital statistics card in the California State Library.)

129

SACRAMENTO CITY is situated on the east bank of the Sacramento River at the junction of the American River and on the southern side of the latter. It stands in about 83 deg., 35 min., north latitude, and 121 deg., 21 min., west longitude. It is about seventy miles above the mouth of the river Sacramento and one hundred and twenty-five miles from San Francisco.

The territory on which the city is located was settled by John A. Sutter in March, 1839. The fort erected by him was commenced the same year. The main walls and buildings of the fort are still standing within the city limits, but the walls of the adjoining enclosures have all been removed and most of the ditches filled up.

The gold was discovered by Marshall on the South Fork of the American River at what is now Coloma in the month of February. In January, 1849, Capt. Warner surveyed and laid off the city plot. The streets run at right angles and are all eighty feet wide except M Street, the center street of the plot, which is one hundred feet. The alleys which divide the blocks are all 20 feet wide. The streets which run east and west, or at right angles with the Sacramento River, are designated by the letters of the alphabet, street A beginning at a point on the American River and the others coming in order through the alphabet. The streets that run north and south, or parallel with the Sacramento River, are designated by numbers, beginning with First or Front Street, along the bank of the river Sacramento, and extending back to Thirty-first Street beyond the fort. The blocks are 320 by 400 feet, divided by 20 foot alleys running east and west.

BUILDINGS

The first building in the city was erected by Samuel Brannan and completed on the first of January, 1849. This building still stands on the corner of Front and J streets and is now two years old. In the spring of 1849 the warehouse of Hensley, Reading & Co. was built on the corner of Front and I streets, where it still remains. The store of Priest, Lee & Co. was erected about the same time and is still left in the block on the corner of Second and J streets, opposite the Eldorado These are the only wood buildings of any size built before August, 1849, and still standing. The City Hotel was quite a notability in its day. The frame of it is that which was to have been erected for a flouring mill on the American River near what is now Brighton—which was brought here after that project was abandoned, and put up on what was once a cornfield. It was finished in September, 1849, and is still to be found flourishing on Front Street between I and J. Till the completion of die City Hotel, the St. Louis Exchange, situated on Second Street between I and J, a rough board building, had been the principal hotel of the city. Later, McKnight's American Hotel, on K Street between Second and Third, where now appears the sign of "Rest for the Weary and Storage for Trunks," did a very thriving business. During the months of September, October, and November, 1849, the number of buildings erected was quite large. Among the largest were the Zinc Warehouse, near the outlet of Lake Sutter; the Zinc House and the Empire, in J Street between Front and Second; Merritt's brick building on the corner of J and Second streets; the Sutter House on Front Street between K and L; the brick block on Front Street between N and O; the Irving House, now the Missouri

Hotel, in J Street between Third and Fourth; and Haycock's building on the corner of J and Fifth streets, then quite out of town.

The principal streets now occupied with buildings are Front Street from D to P; Second Street from Ito P; Third Street from Ito M; Fourth Street from I to L; Fifth Street from I to L; Sixth Street from H to L; Seventh Street from H to M; Eighth Street, from H to M; Ninth Street from I to M; Tenth Street from I to M; Eleventh Street from I to M; Twelth Street from I to M; and Thirteenth to Eighteenth Streets from J to K and L; I Street from Front to Ninth; J Street from Front to Nineteenth; K Street from Front to Thirteenth; L Street from Front to Twelfth; M, N, 0, and P streets from Front to Fourth.

———

MUNICIPAL AFFAIRS

During the first few months of its existence there was no organized government in the town.

On the first of August, 1849, the people of the city, in common with all in the region, voted for delegates to the Convention, which had been called to meet in Monterey and which framed the state constitution. On the same day they chose a TownCouncil and other officers, as follows:

Councilmen J. P. ROGERS, H. E. ROBINSON, P. B.CORNWALL, WM. STOUT, R. GILLESPIE, T. C. CHAPMAN. A. M. WINN, M. T. MCCLELLAN, B. JENNINGS.

J. H. HARPER. Clerk.	J. A. THOMAS. First Magistrate.
B. HANNAH. Sheriff.	J. C. ZABRISKIE. Second do.

The city was chartered by the people on the 13th of October, 1849. A charter previously presented had been voted down. On the 18th of March, 1850, the city was duly incorporated by an act of the State Legislature. The first election under the new charter was held on the 1st of April, 1850, and resulted in the choice of the following persons:

Mayor — HARDIN BIGELOW, formerly of Michigan.
Recorder ---B. F. WASHINGTON, " " Virginia.
Marshal — N. C. CUNNINGHAM, " " Missouri.
Assessor — J. W. WOODLAND, " " Louisiana.

JESSE MOORE, of Wisconsin,
D. STRONG, of New York,
C. A. TWEED, of Florida,
THOMAS MCDOWELL, of N. J.,
V. SPALDING, of Louisiana,   } Councilmen
J. M. MACKENZIE, of Ohio,
CHARLES MILLER, of Conn.,
A. P. PETIT, of Kentucky,
J. R. HARDENBERGH, of N. J.,

133

VESSELS AND STEAMERS

Prior to the founding of the city, schooners and other small craft had visited these parts, mainly for the purpose of procuring hides. At high water they have passed through the outlet and tied up on the bank of Lake Sutter.

The first square-rigged vessel that ever came up to the city was the *Eliodora*, which arrived in March, 1849. Capt. R. Gelston here moored his bark, the *Whiton*, about the first of May; this was the first cargo of merchandise direct from the Atlantic coast.

Ere midsummer there were as many as twenty vessels lying constantly at the levee.

From June to September there was a regular line of schooners running to and from San Francisco; and on these the U. S. mail was carried once a week. The times of arrival and departure were about as uncertain as the payment of debts now is in California.

From September till the rains began, the mail was carried on horseback to Benicia where it took to the water again. By December the steamers were employed in the mail transportation — but the expresses had all the business.

The first craft that came up the river propelled by steam was a small flat-bottomed affair, built at Benicia by the company that came out in the *Edward Everett*. she had no particular name but was usually called the *Washington*. As she came up, rippling the bosom of the placid waters as they slept in their beauty, she was hailed with cheers at every place where there was a tent or shanty; and having sent back a response, on she went puffing and wheezing with all her might with her little high-pressure engine. She reached this place on the 11th of

August, a day and a half from Benicia, having "tied up" over night. She was immediately sold, and ran during the rest of the season between this city and Vernon, when at last she was used up

The *Sacramento* was put on the river in September. She ran as far as New York and there transferred her passengers to sail vessels, the James L. Day and others. The Sacramento is now plying as a ferryboat between this city and Washington.

The *Mint* also made several trips on this river in September and October, as did also some other steamers of diminutive proportions, about which we cannot be precise. It was a great day when about the loth of October the *McKim* first touched at our landing. Speeches were made, cannon boomed, and shouts rent the air. A month later came the *Senator*, with all her speed, pride, and magnificence, and the hearts of the people were satisfied. Steamcraft of all sorts from that time have continued to multiply till their name is legion.

———

WEATHER

The months of August and September, 1849, were excessively hot, the thermometer usually rising above 100° in the shade. There was a slight sprinkle of rain one morning about the last of August. It rained nearly the whole of the afternoon of the 10th of October, 1849.

The rainy season began on the 2d of November, and during the three days following there fell five inches of water.
From the Loth of November onward for six days there fell seven inches of water.

From November 20th to December 2d there were several bright days — nights frosty — some ice formed.

On the 18th of December there came on a very heavy blow which prostrated many tents and buildings, among the rest the frame of what is now the Tehama Block, corner of J and Front streets.

During the month of December rain fell to the depth of fifteen inches, and the rivers all ran full.

Dec. 20th. Thermometer, at noon, 55°.

By Christmas the water was over the lower portions of the city. And on Sunday, the 3oth of December, there were ferries arranged for crossing the sloughs in several of the streets; and the year 1849 closed gloomily.

After the first of January, 1850, the rains ceased a few days, and the water receded a few inches. But in the evening of the 8th of January it commenced storming again. The winds and rains were exceedingly violent. The waters began to rise rapidly. The river and lake overflowed their banks. Ere night of Wednesday, the 9th, four-fifths of the city were under water, and boats were seen all about the streets.

On Thursday there was no dry land in town except at the knoll on the public square near Tenth Street. The water continued rising till Saturday, the 12th of January, 1850, when it came to a stand. That evening there was a clear and beautiful sunset succeeded by a night of stars. The thermometer, at sundown, 54°, and turning colder.

The water commenced receding on the 14th, Monday, and continued to abate slowly until Sunday, the 20th, when portions of the city were getting dry. Thermometer down to 42 °

Feb. 1st. Pleasant weather, clear and mild. Thermometer standing at 66° at noon. Nearly the whole month warm and dry.

Sunday, April 7th, was rainy — the second flood came on — the water began to run into town.

Monday, the 8th. The Council voted money for a temporary levee, and the work went on vigorously under the personal superintendence of Mayor Bigelow. By constant watching and repairing, day and night for a week, the water was kept out of the city, except that which backed up from below.

The last rain fell on the 8th of April, when there were both thunder and hail. During the whole rainy season water fell to the depth of 42 inches.

On Wednesday, June 12th, there was a shower of rain, with thunder and lightning.

Most of the summer was pleasant and agreeable, a fresh cool breeze springing up every afternoon.

Friday and Saturday, 29th and 3oth of August,1850, were about the hottest days — the thermometer at 98° and 100 ° in the shade and 130° in the sun.

During the first two weeks of September there were many cool days. A heavy shower of rain occurred on Sunday evening, the r5th of September, I850.

Tuesday night, November 14th, 1850, the rainy season began. The storm very violent. Several buildings blown down, and considerable damage done.

About I1/2 inches of rain fell in November; and about 1 ¾ inches fell during the month of December, now gone by. Weather for the last three weeks most delightful.

FORMATION OF CHURCHES

The First Church of Christ (Presbyterian, &c.) was organized on the 16th of September, 1849

Grace Church (Episcopal) was organized about the 25th of September, 1849.

The first Baptist Church was organized in November, 1849.

The M. E. Church was formed in the month of October, 1849. The M. E. Church, South, was begun about the month of July, 1850. The first M. E. Church for the colored race was started in August, 1850.

The Roman Catholic Church was organized in the month of October, 1850.

There was no church building erected till November, 1849. Previous to that time there was but one congregation in the city. Stated preaching was commenced as early as June, 1849. The meetings were sometimes held under cover and in new buildings but more commonly beneath the shades of the lofty oaks and sycamores that then graced our city with their venerable presence but have now disappeared forever. At these meetings Rev. Messrs. Deal, Cook, Benton, Owen, and others officiated in turn until November when the Methodist people went into their church; there were then two meetings kept up until the flood when there was again but one. As spring opened all the churches then in existence began to hold separate meetings, each having its own clergyman; and they have so continued till the present time.

———

MISCELLANEOUS

Oct. 1st, 1849 — the population of the city was about 2,000. Wood buildings, 45; cloth houses and tents, Soo; and about 300 campfires, &c., in the open air and under trees.

The mortality rate in the city was very great during November, 1849, reaching some days to the number of 20.

By the first of December, 1849, the population was about 3,50o.

The Fourth of July, 1850, was celebrated by the Sons of Temperance, out in their regalia

On the 14th of August, 1850, there was a conflict between a body of the "Settlers" under arms and the authorities of the city, also armed, during which four persons were killed. Of this number one was Maloney, the leader of the band of "Settlers," and another, J. W. Woodland, the City Assessor, who was a most estimable citizen. Mayor Bigelow was most dangerously wounded.

On Wednesday, September 4th, 1850, occurred the ceremony of laying the cornerstone of the First Church of Christ, in Sixth Street.

On Thursday, September 5th, 1850, took place the funeral ceremonies in grief for the death of Zachary Taylor, President of the United States.

On Sunday, October 14th, 1850, was laid the cornerstone of the Roman Catholic Church.

The ravages of the cholera began in the city about the 15th of October; the epidemic increased in malignity till the first of November, when it was at its height; there were 60 persons buried on that day. After the 5th of November the pestilence rapidly abated and by the 15th had nearly disappeared Within our limits about 500 fell victims to its rage, not all of them our citizens.

Hon. Hardin Bigelow, Mayor of this city, having died of cholera while sojourning at San Francisco, was buried in this city with public honors on the 28th of November, 1850.

The present population of the city consists of about 7,000 permanent and 3,000 transient people. No place could be more healthy than ours has been the last six weeks

———

PUBLIC IMPROVEMENTS

There are only two, as undertaken by the city in its corporate capacity: the levee and the Market House.

Two years have passed since Sacramento City was surveyed and laid off. A portion of the city plot had been previously under cultivation, but the greater part was still in its native wildness and beauty. Majestic oaks and sycamores flourished upon it, now throwing their shadows on the green turf of open parks and now towering like giants above dense, dark thickets and rank undergrowths.

A close observer, even in the dry season, could not fail to notice the evidence of former overflows as exhibited by the marks on the bark of trees, the character of the low shrubbery, and the conformation of the ground. There were stories, too, afloat of men having sailed over the city plot, and the whole valley having been like a lake. There were wooden pins shown, also, driven into trees, five, eight, and ten feet from the ground, said to indicate the height of previous floods.

But the great mass were still incredulous. They would not believe such floods possible. Yet the demonstration came. In January, 1850, the water rose to the highest marks anywhere found of other floods, and the city was suddenly inundated. The early and copious rains of November and December, '49, the unprecedented falls of snow in the mountains, combined with the warm weather and violent storms of January, hurried a deluge of water upon the city and over the whole valley. It was no doubt an extraordinary flood, as the season was a most unusual one.

Yet it may have been well for Sacramento that it was such. For it impelled them to a work of vast moment at once, when an ordinary season might not have convinced them of the necessity of protecting the city from overflow; and then when the disaster in its worst form came, it would have been destructive to the last degree.

To the flood of 1850, in part, we owe it that we have now a levee. Vigorous measures were adopted last spring for carrying forward the work; but it was not finally commenced until about the tenth of September, 1850. Labor at that time was comparatively cheap, otherwise the circumstances were unfavorable. Many of the people had grown indifferent. Some refused to give the right of way. There was no money in the treasury. Loans were hard to obtain. Yet the work went ahead, as few such works have ever gone.

To the untiring industry and energy of Irwin, Gay & Co., the contractors, to the scientific skill of Mr. Binney, the engineer, and to the very able and skilful management of J. R. Hardenbergh, Esq., chairman of the Levee Committee, who superintended the work, are the people indebted for the rearing of this wall of defense around their homes and marts of trade. To all human appearance another inundation is impossible.

The levee thus completed is nine miles in length Beginning at the highlands near Brighton, and thence along the American River to its mouth, the levee is about three feet in height, six feet broad on the top, and twelve at the base. From the mouth of the American River along the Sacramento, and in front of the city, the embankment is raised from three to six feet, being fourteen feet broad on the top and thirty at the base From the river bank to the heights back of Sutter, the most expensive section, the embankment is seventy feet wide at the base and twenty at the top, and is raised from fifteen to twenty feet above the natural surface of the country. In the construction of the work there have been 37 acres of land cleared off and 4,000 square rods grubbed. There have been 750 cubic yards of earth puddled, 4,800 cubic yards excavated, and 121,000 cubic yards made into embankment. The whole cost of the work can not fall much short of one hundred and seventy thousand dollars.

Long may it remain as the monument of our enterprise! No other city of its population has ever completed so grand a work within the first two years of its existence as Sacramento.

The Market House is situated in the center of M Street, between Second and Third. It is built of brick, of the following dimensions: 30 x 110 feet.

The building commenced in the month of October and is now completed. The upper story will be used for municipal purposes.

———

CHURCH BUILDINGS

The Methodist Episcopal Church, North, and parsonage were built in autumn of 1849 at an expense of about $8,000. The church is 24 by 36 feet, with 14-foot posts.

The Methodist Episcopal Church, South, and parsonage, were built in September, 1850, costing about $5,000. The church is 24 by 40 feet, with 16-foot posts.

The Methodist Episcopal Church, for the colored race, and parsonage, were built in September, 1850, costing about $3,000. The church is 20 by 30, 2-foot posts.

The First Church of Christ, and parsonage, in Sixth Street, were completed in October, 1850, at an expense of about $9,000. The church is 36 by 6o feet, with 20-foot posts, and tower of 20 feet.

The Roman Catholic Church, now nearly completed, will cost about $8,000. The church is 30 by 50 feet, with 16-foot posts. The style is gothic.

————

TAXES PAID IN SACRAMENTO

The first taxes assessed for city, county, and state purposes amounted to four and a half per cent. Below is a list of the largest amounts paid:

	City	Co. & State	Aggregate
Barton Lee.	$16,253.12	$6,000	$22,253
J. A. Sutter, Jr., sold to S. Brannan & Co.		14,605.85	5,200
19,805			

	City	Co. & State	Aggregate
S. Brannan	5,354.		
P. H. Burnett	1,571.50	1 15	467
Burnett, Ferguson & Co.	8,896.12	5,0 '	
Bezar Simmons	3,573.50	2,000	5,573
Mellus, Howard & Co.	3,657.50	1,600	5,257
W. M. Carpenter	3,104.50	800	3,904
Maynard, Peachy & Co.	4,048.25	1,300	5,348
H. E. Robinson	3,14445	1,000	4,144
E. F. Gillespie	2,014.24	1,000	3,014
R. J. Watson	1,820.00	800	2,620
J. R. Snyder	1,808.97	700	2,508
Manuel Prieto	1,680.00	475	2,655
Hanner, Jennings & Co.	1,575.00	700	2,275
P. B. Reading	1,660.75	370	2,030
Roland Gelston	1,232.00	600	1,832

	City	Co. & State	Aggregate
S. J. Hensley	1,172.50	450	1,622
Jesse Haycock	1,190.00	325	1,515
Jesse S. Hambleton	1,085.oo	300	1,385
E. Scott	1,067.50	300	1,367
L. Maynard	1,020.25	400	1,420
Isaac T. Mott	971.25	300	1,271
C. H. Soule	927.50	275	1,202
Starr, Bensley & Co.	910.0o	475	1,385
R. A. Pearis	808.50	500	1,308
Paul, White & Co.	1,050.00	350	1,400
Samuel Norris (country) .	892.50	1,800	2,692
Demas Strong	717.50	300	1,017
C. W. Coote	624.75	350	974
James Queen	682.50	300	982

INDEX

first editor and proprietor
of *The California State
Medical Journal,* 21
first vice-president and
orator of Sacramento
Medico-Chirurgical
Academy, 19
forms co-partnership
with Dr. W. R.
Cluness, 17
illness and death, 24
inaugurates system of
health insurance, 14
instrumental in forming
State Agricultural
Society, 21
interest in Sacramento
Valley and Central
Pacific railroads, 19
joins faculty of Toland
Medical College, 24
lodge affiliations, 10, 14,
18
marries Caroline Loney,
17
member of firm of
Warbass & Co., 15
member of the firm of
Morse & Mitchel, 16
member of Volunteer
Fire Department, 23
mining experience, 11
moves to San Francisco,
17

president of California
Prison Commission,
23
president of Sacramento
Society of California
Pioneers, 23
professor of medicine at
University of the
Pacific, 23
school trustee, 23
second vice-president of
Sacramento Medical
Society, 20
settles in Sacramento, 12
tragic death of wife
Rebecca, 16
trustee of California State
Library, 23
Morse, Nellie (daughter of
Dr. John Frederick
Morse, 24
Morse, Rebecca L. Canmore
(first wife of Dr. John
Frederick Morse), 10, 17
Mott, Isaac T., 144
Mount Olivet Cemetery, 25
Mowe, George W., 19
Murray & Lappeas
(Lappeus), 32
Mutual Hook and Ladder
Company No. 1, 123
Myles, Dr., 67
Nevett & Co., 84
Nevett, J. H., 122
New Helvetia, 72

Robinson, Dr. Charles L.,
69, 70, 98, 99, 100, 101,
102
Robinson, Henry E., 53, 66,
83, 127, 133, 144
Robinson, Tod, 123
Rodgers (Rogers), John P.,
53, 94, 133
Rogers, Mr., 66
Round Tent, 43, 45
Rowe's Olympic Circus, 14
Russell, Andrew, 16
Sackett, Charles C., 84, 100
Sacramento Book Collectors
Club, 4, 5, 94
Sacramento City Cemetery,
69
Sacramento Society for
Medical Improvement, 20
Sacramento Society of
California Pioneers, 23
Sacramento Valley Railroad,
4
Sadgett & Co.,, 32
Salaries, 39
Salt Lake, City of, 121
Sanders, Lewis, Jr., 125
Sandwich Islands, 18
Scott, E., 144
Scranton & Smith, 84
Shakespeare reading, 19
Shepherd, Prof. F., 49
Shingleberger, Francis W.
(husband of Nellie
Morse), 24
Simmons, Bezar, 144
Simmons, Hutchinson &
Co., 83

Slater, Peter, 36
Smith, C. C. & Co., 31
Smith, N. E., 66
Snyder, Jacob Rink, 35, 36,
66, 102, 144
Society of California
Pioneers, 19
Sons of Temperance, 139
Soule, C. H., 144
Southard, Charles G., 36
Spalding & Johnson, 127
Spalding & Martin, 84
Spalding, Dr. Volney, 86,
87, 107, 122, 133
Squatter Riots, 70, 93, 139
Squatterism, 112
St. Louis Exchange, 53, 54,
55, 131
Stanford, 19
Stanford & Brothers, 17
Stanford & Brothers', 19
Stanford University Medical
School, 24
Stanford, Leland, 19, 23
Stanley, J., 87
Stark, James the tragedian,
18
Stark, Mrs. James, 73
Starr, Bensley & Co., 83,
144
Starr, Col. James B., 66, 83
Starr, J. B. & Co., 83
State Agricultural Society,
22
Steamboating, 40, 73, 74,
134
Steamboats
Antelope, 75

154

Tweed, Charles A., 86, 89, 95, 107, 133

University of California, Medical Dept., 24

University of the Pacific, 17, 24

Van Houghton, John, 84

Van Pelt, Capt. John, 73, 74

Van Pelt, Charles, 74

Vernon, Town of, 135

Volcano, Town of, 129

Wages, 51

Wakeman, Capt. Edgar, 75

Warbass & Co, 15, 91, 92

Warbass, Thomas A., 15

Warner, Capt. William H., 130

Warner, William H., 30, 32, 129

Warren & Co, 22

Warren, James Lloyd Lafayette, 21, 83, 124

Washington, Benjamin Franklin, 86, 94, 102, 104, 109, 133

Washington, Town of, 73, 135

Watson, R. J., 66, 144

Watson, William H., 122

Webster, Daniel, 124

Welborn, Lambert, 125

Wells, Marion, 25

Wheeler, Rev. Osgood Church, 49

Whig Central Committee, 23

White, Dr. Thomas J., 58, 65, 66, 69, 78

White, William S., 121, 125

Whitney, Dr. James Porter, 24

Wilcoxson & Co., 84

Wilkes, Lieut. Charles, 38

Willis, Judge Edward J., 95, 96, 97, 98, 99, 104

Wilson, Luzena Stanley, 47

Wilson, Robert Anderson, 58, 98

Winans, Joseph William, 124

Wingard, (Wingered), Jacob B., 73

Winn, Albert Mayer, 53, 55, 64, 65, 84, 101, 107, 108, 133

Woodbridge, Rev. Sylvester, 46

Woodland, James Ward, 86, 101, 104, 110, 133, 139

Yosemite Valley, 23

Youmans, Mr., 84

Youngs, Samuel, 125

Yuba River, 40

ZABRISKIE, COL. JAMES CARMEN,, 133

Zinc House, 131

Zinc Warehouse, 131

Zins, George, 31

www.ingramcontent.com/pod-product-compliance
Lightning Source LLC
Chambersburg PA
CBHW060048100426
42742CB00014B/2734